I0408254

The 2016 Elections & The Crisis of American Liberalism

Essays on American Politics in the Era of Trump

By Caleb T. Maupin
Journalist & Political Analyst

Caleb Maupin

Caleb T. Maupin

CONTENTS

The Aftermath

ACKNOWLEDGMENTS

I would like express my appreciation to Alex Kalmikov, Priya Reddy, Mnar Muhawesh, Mikala Reasbeck, Ramiro S. Funez, Dakotah Lilly, Tony Murphy, Bill Dores, Marzieh Hashemi, Ali Merhabi, Justin & Thea Wooten, George Ehrhart, Joe Gale, Michael Lebron, Lynne Shaw, Maria Mercedes Rosales-Maupin, William Camacaro, Paul Sheppard, Patrick Scanlan, Lucy & Roberto Quesada, and everyone else who assisted me in writing and proof-reading the articles contained within this volume, provided useful feedback or insights, or inspired or directed me toward deeper political analysis and global understanding.

INTRODUCTION:
JULY 4TH, 2015 - SETTING THE
STAGE

July 4th, 2015 - RT.com

"If you could separate causes from results, if you could know that Paine, Marx, Jefferson, Lenin were results, not causes, you might survive,"
-    John Steinbeck, "The Grapes of Wrath," 1939

Its the Fourth of July in America, and gay marriage has just been legalized by a Supreme Court ruling, the Confederate flag is being displayed on public property and Black churches are being set afire.

Meanwhile, the police continue to kill African Americans without accountability. The government has developed flying killer robots that are able to assassinate people from the sky. The

National Security Agency is recording the phone calls, emails, and internet activities of millions of US citizens. Beyond American borders, our leaders are psyching us up for bigger confrontations with Russia and China, as US military forces pour into the Pacific.

The above paragraphs sound like the opening of an apocalyptic science fiction novel. However, it's all true. And it gets worse.

The Angry, Poor Millennials Are Getting Political

Underlying it all is an economic crisis. The so-called "recovery" has missed a big section of the country. The good-paying industrial jobs that once defined the US "middle class" have been eliminated. Young people with record amounts of student debt are stuck in a low-wage economy, often living off their parents. US popular discourse bemoans this generation of "millennials" who "just can't get their lives together." Young mid-Westerners and Southerners are fleeing to the coastal areas in order to find jobs. Life in much of the Rust Belt has simply become unlivable.

Despite not being as inclined to buy houses and cars or get married at the rate of previous generations, the young millennials seem to be far more interested in politics. In 2011, they slept in tents around the clock at Occupy camps protesting the power of the wealthy "1 percent." Now, a few years later, young millennials are shutting down highways and bridges in opposition to police brutality, as the new rallying cry is "Black Lives Matter!" The increasingly active new generation of low-paid workers with student debt is much more favorable to once forbidden political ideologies like socialism. Libertarianism, anarchism and communism all have a slew of new adherents as well.

In the background, starting just a little more than a week after the July 4 holiday, the US military will begin a series of military exercises in the southwestern states codenamed "Operation Jade Helm," which has been explained to the public as rehearsal for "unconventional warfare" on US soil. "Unconventional warfare" is military-speak for armed insurrections among the population. The US Army Green Berets, US Marines Special Operation Command, US Navy Seals, and US Air Force Special Operations Command will be in nine different states practicing "counterinsurgency" tactics.

"The Battle Cry of Freedom"

As much as all of the above sounds shocking, I'm not deeply perturbed. History is the most flunked and disliked subject among students in the United States. The reason students in the US don't like to learn history is because they are taught a very dull and patriotic version of events.

If we actually knew the history of the North American continent, we would all see that the political drama and rising unrest of the last decade fits into a historical pattern of repression, struggle and resistance.

Take the latest controversy: the Confederate flag. This is not the symbol of southerners who think New Englanders look down on their accents. That was the flag chosen to represent a group of states who attempted to withdraw from the country in response to the election of a third-party candidate.

The Republican Party was a stronghold of radicals and rabble-rousers back in the 1860s. It took its name from the radical "Republican" movements of Europe. Its supporters unfurled bright red flags. The Republican Party newspaper of New York City, the New York Tribune, hired Karl Marx as its London correspondent. Radical Christian abolitionists such as John Brown launched armed attacks on the US government. Among the slaves themselves, there were constant uprisings and rebellions.

In 1852, Frederick Douglass, who later became a prominent leader of the Republican Party, shamed a crowd of people for inviting him to a Fourth of July celebration.

He thundered, "What, to the American slave, is your 4th of July? I answer: a day that reveals to him, more than all other days in the year, the gross injustice and cruelty to which he is the constant victim. To him, your celebration is a sham; your boasted liberty, an unholy license; your national greatness, swelling vanity; your sounds of rejoicing are empty and heartless; your denunciations of tyrants, brass fronted impudence; your shouts of liberty and equality, hollow mockery; your prayers and hymns, your sermons and thanksgivings, with all your religious parade, and solemnity, are, to him, mere bombast, fraud, deception, impiety, and hypocrisy — a thin veil to cover up crimes which would disgrace a nation of savages. There is not a nation on the earth guilty of practices, more shocking and bloody, than are the people of these United States, at this very hour."

Abraham Lincoln took office on a platform of refusing to allow slavery to expand into the Western territories. In response, the wealthy slave plantation owners decided to secede from the country. They had the support of Wall Street, which was making lots of money insuring and loaning money to the slave owners and otherwise making profits from human bondage. The Confederates also had the support of the richest people within the British Empire, who saw slave plantations as a source of cheap cotton for the emerging textile industry.

The Confederate flag was unfurled to defend the practice of owning human beings as property. The secession of the slave owners provoked a mass mobilization of the people. Labor unions mobilized their members to join the fight. Harriet Tubman led a battalion of former slaves and union soldiers through South Carolina, raiding and liberating the plantations along the Combahee River. Also leading the battle against the slave owners was German immigrant August Willich, who commanded the famous Ohio 9th Infantry Regiment. Willich was openly and proudly a Communist who corresponded with Karl Marx throughout the war. The Ohio 9th unfurled the Red Flag as its officials colors, and sang the "La Marseilles" anthem of the French Revolution as they marched into battle.

What we have all been told was a "war between the states" in history classes and dull Ken Burns' documentaries on PBS was in reality a massive people's revolution. Wall Street, the British Empire, and the rich slave plantation owners were defeated by a broad coalition of everyday Americans who were sick and tired of them. The coalition that defeated the slavocracy included slave rebels, labor activists, radical Christians and even some communists. The song that rallied this broad coalition of anti-slavery revolutionaries was called "The Battle Cry of Freedom."

Revolutions and mass rebellions are not foreign to the United States. The country began with an uprising against the British Empire. The heralded Boston Tea Party was a mass act of property damage and vandalism. The Bill of Rights only ended up in the US Constitution after popular outcry demanded it.

In modern times, the reason we have Social Security, unemployment insurance and paved roads in the suburbs is because of mass rebellions and the unemployed during the 1930s. The Unemployment Councils fought the police to prevent evictions during the Great Depression. Their slogan was: "Don't Starve, Fight!" The government responded to the wave of street battles by hiring the unemployed into the Works Progress Administration.

President Franklin Delano Roosevelt, who aligned with this mass movement of low-income people, described what they were rebelling against. He said: "We had to struggle with the old enemies of peace - business and financial monopoly, speculation, reckless banking, class antagonism, sectionalism, war profiteering. They had begun to consider the government of the United States as a mere appendage to their own affairs. We know now that government by organized money is just as dangerous as government by organized mob."

The United States currently has an African American president because of generations of struggle against racism. Martin Luther King, Jr. now has a national holiday in his honor, but once US television declared him to be Soviet agent and a traitor because he actively fought for civil rights and racial equality. This man, now loved and commemorated throughout US society, spent many days sitting inside the country's jails. The FBI tracked him everywhere he went, and urged him to commit suicide with threatening letters.

In the last years of his life, King himself even declared: "There must be better distribution of wealth and maybe America must move toward a democratic socialism. Call it what you may, call it democracy, or call it democratic socialism, but there must be a better distribution of wealth within this country for all of God's children."

Mass protests and rebellions against the tyranny of big bankers and government acting as their hired stooges are nothing new. The blood of radicals and revolutionaries who fought against injustice, often using the latest Second Amendment technology, flows through the veins of all who reside on US soil.

Even slave-owning Thomas Jefferson, who has been eulogized as an iconic "founding father," was enthusiastic about the perpetuation of massive uprisings in the country he helped establish. He stated bluntly: "What country can preserve its liberties if their rulers are not warned from time to time that their people preserve the spirit of resistance? Let them take arms… The tree of liberty must be refreshed from time to time with the blood of patriots and tyrants. It is its natural manure."

Compared to Thomas Jefferson, Frederick Douglass, Martin Luther King, Jr., and Franklin Roosevelt, many of the newly politicized youth of today seem somewhat conservative. In general, all they have asked for with their wave of peaceful protests and occupations is some accountability from police officers, government officials, and the people who run the economy. In terms of US history, they have shown a great amount of restraint.

What's Next?

The wages and standard of living in the United States is going down. The police are escalating their brutality against African Americans and getting away with it. Our much cherished civil liberties are being stripped away. Cops and prisons are everywhere, but good-paying jobs are vanishing. So, what happens next?

The people of the United States, especially the next generation so decried as "lazy," is resuming the forgotten traditions of struggle against the rich and powerful. They are filling the streets. They are remembering who "The American People" really are and what they are capable of.

Many have decided to put down their Playstations and take up "The Battle Cry of Freedom." Wall Street's blueprint for a low-wage prison is being repudiated, not only with tweets and Facebook *"likes,"* but with concrete action.

The forces responsible for the currently disastrous state of affairs are not in Caracas, Pyongyang, Moscow, Damascus or Tehran. The tyrants on this Independence Day are much closer to home - on Wall Street and in Washington, DC.

If the schemes of this ruling elite push the country into some foreign war, this could be their fatal error. Less than 50 years ago during the Vietnam War, soldiers were fragging their officers and refusing to fight. Students were taking over buildings and burning their draft cards. The recent escalation of US military presence in the Pacific, and the campaign of demonization being waged against Russia and China, could backfire on the billionaires and warmongers. If things get out of hand internationally, they are more likely to see great upheaval from the "lazy millennials" than any enthusiasm or willingness to go fight for Wall Street against a major world power.

Call me a conspiracy theorist, but I don't think the military drills dubbed "Operation Jade Helm" are about rehearsing for battle against ISIS or Al-Qaeda. I think the boys in Washington and their bosses on Wall Street know US history pretty well.

They know that "We, the People" won't let them get away with this stuff for very much longer. The United States isn't frozen in time. The actions of tyrants often have unpredictable consequences. History will keep marching forward, whether or not they choose to get onboard.

Part One:
Clinton
Controversies

CLINTON'S HYPOCRISY:

US LEADERS FREQUENTLY INTERVENE IN FOREIGN ELECTIONS

March 8th, 2016 - New Eastern Outlook

The US media is nearly foaming at the mouth with unsubstantiated allegations that Russia is attempting to influence US elections. The words of commentators on mainstream US media are, "How dare Russia try to influence our elections!" and "How dare Putin meddle in the affairs of other countries!"

Beyond the lack of actual evidence to back up these claims, there is a layer of absolute hypocrisy. For decades leaders of the United States have been actively trying to influence the elections of other countries in a way that is favorable to the centers of American economic power. Often, this meddling is also done to prevent the election of governments who are sympathetic to Russia or China.

The stated purpose of the "Marshall Plan" enacted by the United States after the Second World War was to weaken Moscow-aligned political forces across the world. US leaders put pressure on various governments to suppress Communist parties, even when they were wildly popular and won at the polls. In 1947, when Communists were pushed out of the cabinet, the World Bank rewarded France with a loan, just hours afterward.

In China the United States supported the Nationalist government in barring the Communist Party from participating in the post-war elections. In response to being barred from the ballot, the Communists took up arms and eventually created the People's Republic of China in 1949.

In Korea, the United States coopered with forces who made sure that the post-war elections, which would likely have elected Soviet- aligned forces, never took place. Instead of the planned national election for the entire Korean Peninsula, the US supported General Sygman Rhee in establishing a military dictatorship in the south. With full US support Rhee slaughtered tens of thousands of leftists at Jeju Island and elsewhere.

In Italy and other countries throughout Europe, the United States cooperated with NATO countries to conduct "Operation Gladio" in order to prevent the often wildly popular Communist parties from winning elections. In Italy, the CIA not only facilitated a campaign of media smears and demonization, but also conducted election fraud and staged armed acts of violence, successfully preventing the Italian public from electing a Russian-aligned government. Since the end of the Cold War, it has been revealed that US and other NATO intelligence services were involved in terrorist attacks in which civilians were killed. These acts of terrorism were done with the intention of weakening the Communists at the polls.

These kinds of schemes were conducted by US intelligence agencies throughout the Cold War. In Indonesia, the United States did everything possible to sabotage and discredit the China aligned government of Sukarno. When well-funded attempts to defeat the pro-Chinese coalition government were unsuccessful, the United States backed a military in coup d'etat in 1965. In the aftermath of the military seizing power in Indonesia and toppling Sukarno, hundreds of thousands of people were killed. Some say the mass slaughtered that followed the 1965 coup even escalated beyond political violence and became essentially a genocide against ethnic Chinese people in Indonesia.

In the early 1970s, the United States intentionally worked to sabotage the economy Chile, openly hoping to destabilize the country and discredit the socialist coalition which had been democratically elected. Richard Nixon directly ordered the CIA to "make the economy scream" in order to weaken the popularity of the Socialist Party, which was friendly to the Soviet Union. When efforts to influence the elections failed, the United States supported a military coup d'etat in which Augusto Pinochet seized power, killing thousands of leftists and dissidents.

In 1990, the Sandinista government of Nicaragua held elections. The United States had been funding armed groups known as Contras for over a decade hoping to topple the government. As the elections drew near, the allies of the United States, with millions of dollars to fund their campaign at the ballot box, assured the public that if the Sandinistas were voted out of power, the campaign of terrorism would end. The people of Nicaragua, scarred by years of war, voted for the opposition.

Clinton's Meddling in Elections Across The Planet

Since the rise of Hugo Chavez in Venezuela in 1999, the United States has been actively working to influence the elections in a number of Latin American countries. The US openly cooperates with opposition forces in Venezuela, Bolivia, Ecuador, Nicaragua, El Salvador, and Cuba. The leaked e-mails of Hillary Rodham Clinton reveal that as Secretary of State she worked very hard to influence elections in Latin America and to defeat Bolivarian socialists at the ballot box.

Clinton and other US leaders have actively tried to influence elections and secure the defeat of the elected government of Belarus, led by Alexander Lukashenko. On several occasions when the pro-western minority in Belarus has been defeated at the polls, the streets of the country have experience a wave of violence from US-backed "oppositionists."

Despite Vladimir Putin being one of the most popular heads of state on earth, Clinton has publicly aligned herself with the widely unpopular, pro-western Russian opposition. The US State Department most certainly has a relationship with such forces as well.

The allegation currently plastered across US media is that somehow Russia was involved in making public some e-mails revealing dishonesty and malpractice by the Democratic National Committee. The allegation is that Russia would prefer that Trump rather than Clinton be elected in November, and that making the dishonest activities of Debbie Wasserman Shultz and others public will hurt Clinton's image.

The actions that the Clinton campaign is currently accusing Russia of engaging in are very mild in comparison to what has been actively done by US leaders to influence the elections of other countries. Across the planet, when it was feared that elections may go differently than they preferred, US intelligence agencies have funded terrorist groups, supported people engaged in electoral fraud, and done everything possible to secure the results they want. Often, when countries elect governments they disfavor, the United States has supported military coups that overturned the elected governments.

In the allegations surrounding the US elections, Russia is not being accused of anything remotely close to what US leaders have done to influence the elections of other countries. However, the history of US meddling with elections across the planet is unfortunately absent from mainstream media discourse, allowing a hostile climate of Russophobia to escalate.

CLINTON'S E-MAILS, BIG OIL & THE DANGER OF SECTARIAN WAR

July 10th, 2016 - New Eastern Outlook

On Friday, July 1st, thousands of people peacefully assembled in the streets Zaria, a city in the northern part of Nigeria. The marchers carried banners painted with images of the Dome of the Rock in Jerusalem, as well as placards and flags condemning Israel.

On the last Friday of Ramadan, Muslims across the world take to the street for the "Day of Al-Quds" to protest against Israel, and to demand that "Al-Quds" (also known as Jerusalem) be returned to the Palestinians.

The demonstrations this year in Nigeria, which proceeded peacefully in spite of threats from the military and Boko Haram terrorists, were particularly noteworthy. The demonstrations were organized by the Islamic Movement in Nigeria, but also included Christians, Sunnis, and others who oppose Israeli atrocities. Fearlessly, the Nigerian Al-Quds marchers not only rallied against Israel, but also called for the leader of the Islamic Movement in Nigeria, Sheikh Ibrahim Al-Zakzaky, to be released.

Zakzaky, the top Shia cleric in Nigeria, remains in military detention after being swept up in a raid on his neighborhood. The incident has been called the Zaria Massacre, and has been condemned by a wide variety of voices, including Amnesty International.

At least 300 unarmed civilians were slaughtered on December 12th, 2015 when the Nigerian military attacked the headquarters of the Islamic movement in Nigeria. Sheikh Zakzaky has been held in military detention without any criminal charges filed against him since that day. Many of his sons and daughters were among those who were slaughtered. The Nigerian military now says that Zakzaky is being held, against his will, "for his own protection." The Shia Muslims of Nigeria reject this assertion, and demand his immediate unconditional release.

Clinton E-mails Discuss "Sectarian War" as "Not a Bad Thing"

Just a few days after the Al-Quds demonstrations took place across the world, Shia neighborhoods in Saudi Arabia were rattled with bombs. No one has yet claimed responsibility for these attacks. Within Saudi Arabia, Shia Muslims live as second-class citizens. They are mostly not permitted to become educated, and are forced to work as manual laborers. While the Saudi Royal family lives in luxury, it is Shia Muslims who sweat in the oil fields and refineries, extracting and refining the thousands of barrels exported by the repressive Kingdom every day. The Shia community in Saudi Arabia still boils with rage over the fact that their most high ranking leader, Ayatollah Nimr Al-Nimr, was executed in January.

The Hezbollah organization in Lebanon has had its mosques targeted by ISIS bombs, as its fighters continue to support the Syrian government on the battlefield. Iraqi Shias have faced a wave of terrorism since the US invasion of Iraq. One of the most holy Shia sites, the Al-Askari Mosque, was bombed in 2006, destroying its golden dome. Almost everywhere Shia Muslims are being targeted and killed. The Islamic Republic of Iran, the only country in the world with a government based on Shia Islam, faces a wave of attacks motivated by religious hate.

A terrorist organization called Jindallah operates on Iran's border with Afghanistan, funding its operations by smuggling heroin. The organization was infiltrated by the US Port Authority Police, which refused to notify Iran of pending terrorist attacks against civilians.

On July 4th, 30,000 of Hillary Clinton's e-mails were released by Wikileaks. A number of Clinton's e-mails dealt with Iraq. In some of the e-mails it can be read how Clinton and other state department officials scrambled to protect the residents of "Camp Ashraf" or "Camp Liberty." This is a place in Iraq where the Mujahideen E-Khalq, a legally designated Foreign Terrorist Organization until 2013, based its operations, working to violently topple the Islamic Republic of Iran.

The Mujahideen E-Khalq are terrorists who call themselves "Islamo-Marxists." From their camp in Iraq they have conducted many assassinations and bombings. The most notorious of MEK's recent acts has been assassinating peaceful Iranian scientists in coordination with Mossad.

Hillary Clinton's newly released e-mails show how the elected Iraqi government grew tired of hosting a group of murderous terrorists who were using Iraqi soil as a headquarters for their operations. Clinton and other state department officials negotiated with the Iraqi government, doing everything they could to make sure that the Mujahadeen E-Khalq terrorists, who have killed tens of thousands of innocent civilians over the last three decades, were not arrested and were safely evacuated to a new location.

The United States and Israel, in a close alliance with Saudi Arabia, are actively supporting the killing of Shia Muslims around the world. From the US-backed Nigerian regime, to Yemen, Iraq, and Syria, forces that are actively calling for the slaughter of what they refer to as "Shia Apostates," are receiving sometimes passive and sometimes blatant support.

One of the already leaked Clinton e-mails indicates that US leaders are considering the possible benefits of a sectarian war between Sunni and Shia across the Middle East. An e-mail forwarded to Hillary Clinton about Syria contained the deeply disturbing passage: "The fall of the House of Assad could well ignite a sectarian war between the Shiites and the majority Sunnis of the region drawing in Iran, which, in the view of Israeli commanders would not be a bad thing for Israel and its Western allies."

The hypothetical war discussed by Hillary Clinton's e-mails is not exactly what's happening. It is easy to dismiss the conflict between Sunni and Shia Muslims as another longstanding ethno-religious rivalry. Observers in the West are tempted to repeat commonly heard statements like "these people have been fighting for thousands of years" and, "there is truth on both sides." However, if one looks deeper at the conflict, you can see that these cliches do not apply.

For example, in the Islamic Republic of Iran, led by Shia Muslims, Sunni Muslims are free to openly practice and proselytize their faith, as are Christians, Zoroastrians, and Jews. All believers in monotheism are guaranteed religious freedom under the Iranian constitution, though the government takes a Shia perspective and is lead by Shia clerics.

In Syria, Shia Muslims in Hezbollah and Iran's Revolutionary Guards are standing shoulder to shoulder with Syrian Christians, Communist atheists, and Orthodox Christian Russian Nationalists in order to fight against ISIS. The overwhelming majority of the soldiers in the Syrian Arab Army loyal to the internationally recognized Syrian government, are Sunnis.

In Yemen, the Zaidi Shia Ansarullah organization, also known as the Houthis, is aligned with both Sunnis and Secularists in a Revolutionary Committee to fight against the Saudi-led attack on the country.

Shia Muslims are simply not pushing religious sectarianism in the Middle East. Neither are most

Sunnis. The call for violence against people on the basis of their religious and ethnic background is coming from a specific group of Sunni fanatics who have lots of money behind them.

The campaign of violence, primarily targeting Shia Muslims cannot truly be described as a "Sunni-Shia" conflict. In reality, this is a war on civilization waged by Wahabbi fanatics. The most open targets of the Wahabbi fanatics are Shia Muslims, but many Sunnis and Christians have been slaughtered by them as well. As Wahabbi terrorists get stronger, it is not only the Shia, but Christians, Druze, Yazidis, and even moderate Sunnis who are in great danger.

Big Oil & Wahabbism

Wahabbism is a fanatical interpretation of Sunni Islam started by Muhammad Ibn Al-Wahhab. Wahhab's ideas were embraced by the Saudi monarchy in the 1700s. Beginning in the late 1800s, the British empire began funding and promoting the Saudi Royal family and their ideology of Wahabbism, seeing it as a useful tool against the Ottoman empire. The United States began cooperating with Saudi Arabia and Wahabbism during the Second World War.

The reason the US and British governments promoted and aligned with Wahabbis was obvious: oil. The Arabian Peninsula is one of the most oil-rich regions in the entire world. Only Venezuela has bigger oil deposits than Saudi Arabia, and this was only recently discovered.

The British defeated the Ottoman empire in the First World War. With Saudi Wahabbis as their allies, British bankers like the Rothschilds secured access to the oil of the Middle East region. After the Russian Revolution, the American and Anglo bankers were desperate for oil, because the Soviet Union had taken the Baku oil fields of Azerbaijan out of their hands.

Control of Saudi Arabia's oil was key in securing the allied victory during the Second World War. The Nazis great weakness was their dependence on imported oil to fuel their war machine. Wahabbism began to spread across the planet during the 1970s, as steeper oil prices made Saudi Arabia far wealthier. The CIA aided Osama bin Laden in building a Wahabbi army in Afghanistan to fight against the People's Democratic Party throughout the 1980s. Among those who aligned with the Wahabbi fanatics in Afghanistan was Siddique Mateen, the father of the mass shooter in Orlando.

Two dangerous groups of Wahabbi terrorists now control huge chunks of Syrian territory. The so-called Islamic State Organization (referred to as ISIS or Daesh) describes itself as the most true adherents to the Wahabbi ideology. Another

Wahabbi organization known as the Al-Nusra Front, also controls huge chunks of Syrian territory. Among the so-called "moderate" rebels, the majority are Wahabbis of some variety. It is widely confirmed that Saudi Arabia, as well as some western countries have been actively supporting the Al-Nusra Front. David Petraeus recently testified before Congress that he believed the United States should directly join these efforts, and send guns to Al-Nursa, previously known as Al-Queda in Syria.

Saudi television not only promotes Wahabbism, but fixates on hate for Shia Muslims. Saudi Arabia's propaganda to Muslims around the world preaches that Iran is somehow attempting to establish a "Shia crescent" and to conquer the world into a Shia empire. Saudi propaganda dismisses all the forces resisting Wahabbi terrorism in the Middle East as some kind of vast, Iranian conspiracy, despite the fact that they are one of the most religiously and politically diverse military coalitions in world history, containing Communists, Islamic Revolutionaries, Arab Nationalists, and Christians, which are all united against Wahabbi terrorism.

The Nigerian government that slaughtered Shia Muslims in December, the Saudi-Wahabbi Kingdom, and Hillary Clinton, all have one thing in common: They all work closely with the top US oil companies.

In Yemen, the United States is aligned with Saudi Arabia against a popular democratic uprising involving the People's Coalition & the Ansarullah Organization.

British Petroleum, Royal Dutch Shell, Exxon-Mobile, and Chevron are the four largest oil companies in the world, and are commonly called the "Supermajors." They function almost like a trust or cartel, by coordinating production and pricing with each other. All four of them buy Saudi oil.

Hillary Clinton's personal foundation (along with the Council on Foreign Relations which strategizes for the CIA, and other major US foreign policy think tanks) is openly bankrolled by Exxon-Mobile and other big oil corporations.

The Nigerian government cooperates closely with Shell and Chevron as the top oil- exporting country on the African continent. Shell oil even maintains its own private army in the oil-rich Niger Delta Region. It's no coincidence that

Wahabbi terrorists in "Boko Haram" have been terrorizing people in Nigeria for over a decade. Saudi Arabia's spreading of Wahabbi fanaticism around the world depends on its relationship with big oil corporations on Wall Street. Everywhere big oil goes, Wahabbism is not far behind.

Wahabbi terrorists are working to overthrow the Syrian Arab Republic, a country that cooperates closely with the Islamic Republic of Iran, and had been talking about joint oil pipelines and ventures when the civil war began five years ago. Wahabbi terrorists are working to fight against the democratic uprising in Yemen, and restore the Saudi- backed dictator Mansour Hadi. Wahabbi terrorists have targetted Russia, and even unleashed a wave of stabbings on trains in the People's Republic of China. The targets of Wahabbi fanatics are also the biggest enemies of Wall Street.

The destruction of Libya in 2011 with a NATO bombing campaign, and the toppling of the Islamic Socialist government unleashed Wahabbi forces in the country. Al-Queda and ISIS had almost no presence in Libya before 2011, but since the NATO bombing campaign they have become stronger than ever before. The same can be said for Iraq and Afghanistan. US foreign policies, executed in the name of a "War on Terror," seem to be making Wahabbi terrorists more powerful.

"War of Poverty Against Wealth"

It makes sense that big oil would align itself with fanatics who hate Shia Muslims. Shia Islam, with its message of social justice, and opposition to capitalism, is an enemy of Wall Street.

Shia Muslims honor not just the Prophet Muhammad, but also the Imams who seceded him. Imams Ali and Hussain were martyred in battles against very rich and powerful people. Shia holy days like Ashura commemorate those who sacrificed their lives "for the oppressed." The sayings of Imams Ali and Hussain contain many anti-capitalist and populist sentiments. The last will and testament of Imam Ali instructs Muslims "Do not yearn for the world, and do not be seduced by it. Do not resent anything you have missed in it. Proclaim the truth; work for the next world. Oppose the oppressor and support the oppressed."

The Islamic Revolution of Iran in 1979 took a major oil producing country out of the hands of Wall Street and London. The Shah, who had acted as the puppet of big oil corporations, and lived in splendor as his country remained underdeveloped and impoverished, and was toppled.

The Islamic Republic of Iran came into existence with slogans such as "Neither East Nor West", "Not Capitalism, but Islam", and "War of Poverty

Iran's 1979 Islamic Revolution was won on the basis of the slogans "War of Poverty Against Wealth," "Not Capitalism But Islam," and "Neither East nor West."

Against Wealth." The Islamic Revolution in Iran inspired uprisings of Shia Muslims all across the world. Within Saudi Arabia, Shia oil workers rose up and battled against the Wall Street oil monarchy, inspired by Iran's example.

Shia in Lebanon have formed the militant Hezbollah organization, which acts almost as a commune state, caring for the people and arming them to defend themselves. Hezbollah scored a huge victory against Israeli invaders in 2006. In Nigeria, Pakistan, Lebanon, Iran, Iraq, Saudi Arabia and elsewhere, Shia Muslims are obligated by their faith to stand not just for religious principles, but also for social justice. Within Iran,

one can see government officials who honor
Malcolm X and the Black Liberation Movement
of the United States.

The Iranian government came to the aid of the
Irish Republican Army as it battled against the
British empire in the 1980s. Iran has continued to
aid the Palestinian people in their fight against
Israel, despite much of the Palestinian leadership
being very hostile to them, and their having a
different religious perspective.

The attack on Shia Muslims is done in order to
protect the rich and powerful. Shia Islam has
become a vehicle with which those who long for
stability and social justice can express themselves,
and become organized to fight.

Everyone who values justice and wants an end to
terrorism should be deeply concerned about the
rising persecution of Shia Muslims. The fact that
Hillary Clinton's e-mails show her indifference and
in some cases, direct participation in it, should be
deeply upsetting to morally conscious people
within the United States.

HAS US MEDIA FORGOTTEN THE 1990S?

September 9th, 2016 - New Eastern Outlook

US media is filled with unproven allegations that Russia is working to defeat Hillary Clinton at the polls in November. Despite no solid evidence being provided, Clinton continues to allege that Russia is responsible for the leaking of DNC e-mails, and mainstream media echoes her allegation.

What motive could possibly exist for this alleged crime? According to Clinton it is about ideology. As Clinton put it in her recent speech: "The grand godfather of this global brand of extreme nationalism is Russian President Vladimir Putin." Essentially, Clinton argues that Putin holds similar political views to Trump, and is trying to get him elected.

The unproven allegations based on a rather loose perception of ideological similarities, forces students of American history to recall the Cold War rhetoric of the far- right. For example, Martin Luther King Jr. was frequently called a Soviet agent by the US right-wing simply because both Soviet Communists and the Civil Rights Activists believed in racial equality. In the early 1960s, a widely circulated documentary from Edward G. Griffin purported to "prove" a link between the Civil Rights Movement and the Cuban government because "Venceremos" and "We Shall Overcome" have a similar meaning.

Regardless of unproven allegations and perceived ideological similarities, when discussing Hillary Clinton's Presidential campaign, and Russia, there is an obvious factor that is being left out. It's an entire decade called the 1990s.

Clinton's Man-Made Famine

Americans generally have no idea what life was like for Russians during the 1990s. They naively assume that because Russia swiftly adopted capitalism, the result was great economic prosperity. The reality was quite different.

After the collapse of the Soviet Union, Boris Yeltsin took office and dramatically re-organized Russia's economy on free market lines. When Bill Clinton was elected as President of the United States, it was widely understood that Yeltsin was "Clinton's man." According to the US Bureau of Public Affairs, Boris Yeltsin and Bill Clinton were very close. The official US government website states: "Clinton was strongly inclined not only to like Yeltsin but also to support his policies, in particular, his commitment to Russian democracy." US President Bill Clinton met with Boris Yeltsin 18 times while he was in office.

The US Bureau of Public Affairs goes on to explain exactly how the administration of Bill Clinton pushed Yeltsin's free market policies : "At the time, and periodically throughout his term in office, Yeltsin faced growing opposition at home to his efforts to liberalize the economy and enact democratic reforms in Russia. At Vancouver, Clinton promised Yeltsin strong support in the form of financial assistance to promote various programs, including funds to stabilize the economy… Although not always able to deliver such assistance, Clinton also supported Yeltsin and his position on economic and political matters by other means."

While only 6% of the Russian public approved of Yeltsin's "reforms," the Clinton administration directed and sponsored the Yeltsin administration's efforts in Russia. With the approval of Washington, the International Monetary Fund, and the World Bank, Yeltsin privatized state owned industries, lifted price controls, and in the process left millions of Russians in desperate conditions. US economist Jeffrey Sachs of Columbia University was dispatched to Russia in order to oversee the process.

The result was not the establishment of a free market paradise, but rather a huge catastrophe. US Senator Bill Bradley explained it this way: "30% unemployment, rampant inflation, pensions gone, savings gone, 30 or 40 years... it's all gone. No jobs. A few people doing very well, who bought all assets from the state, but the average person, no." According to Naomi Klein's 2007 book "The Shock Doctrine" between 1991 and 1998 "more than 80 percent of Russian farms had gone bankrupt and roughly seventy thousand state factories had closed creating an epidemic of unemployment." As a result, 74 million Russians were living below the poverty line. Klein goes on to say that "25 percent of Russians – almost 37 million people – lived in poverty described as 'desperate.'"

During the 1990s, when Yeltsin was dramatically changing the country under the direction of the Clinton administration, the rate of drug addiction in Russia increased by 900 percent. The suicide rate almost doubled. HIV, which had previously only infected no more than fifty thousand Russians, became a nationwide epidemic with millions contracting AIDs.

An entire population of people who had lived with guaranteed employment, guaranteed healthcare, old age pensions, and a planned economy saw the social safety net swept from underneath them, as widely unpopular policies, backed by Washington, were imposed on the country. US Senator Bill Bradley describes the tone of US diplomats in their interactions with Russia, saying Clinton administration officials spoke of "stuffing shit down Boris throat," gleefully taking pleasure in ordering him to wreck his country's economy.

Anti-Communist scholars frequently accuse Stalin and other Soviet leaders of creating "man-made famines." Sometimes the anti-communist scholars will say these "man made famines" amounted to "genocide." The words used by many people to describe what US President Bill Clinton and economist Jeffrey Sachs presided over in Russia during the 1990s sound a lot like descriptions of a "man-made famine."

Naomi Klein quotes a Russian Academic named Vladimir Gusev as saying "The years of criminal capitalism have killed off 10 percent of our population." Russia's population decreased by 6.6 million between 1992 and 2006. Klein quotes US

Economist Andre Gunder Frank calling what took place in Russia as "economic genocide." Russian Vice President Alexander V. Rutskoi used the same words as the policies were beginning in 1992, saying it would have catastrophic results for children and the elderly.

Clinton Represents Neo-Liberalism

When people speculate that Russia is intervening in US elections, why is Clinton's record in Russia not discussed? The last time Hillary Clinton was residing in the White House, though only as the first lady, millions of Russians lives were ruined in what some have called an "economic genocide." Is this fact not relevant in discussing Russia and 2016 US Presidential elections?

It has only been since the ascension of Vladimir Putin that the situation in Russia has improved. During the first eight years of Putin's presidency, wages doubled and the poverty rate was reduced by 14%. During this same period Russia experienced overall industrial expansion of more than 70%. The country's Gross Domestic Product increased from $764 billion to $2096.8 billion between 2007 and 2014. John Browne, the CEO of BP has praised Putin's policies saying "No country has come so far, in such a short space of time."

What was the secret to fixing Russia's economy? Putin dropped many of the extreme free market policies that had been championed by Clinton and Yeltsin. Russia's economy re-emerged primarily due to public control of oil and natural gas. The Russian economy is now centered around state controlled natural resources with a very high rate of public ownership. Putin's "National Priorities Project" focused on building a social safety net for the population. The Russian government has also created "Nashi" summer camps, hoping to cultivate and train the best and brightest young Russians to work for the good of their nation.

Despite being described as "left," both Hillary Clinton and her husband are closely identified with neoliberalism and privatizations. Bill and Hillary Clinton's political careers are closely associated with the Democratic Leadership Council, a non-profit organization that maneuvered within the Democratic Party to push for free market policies and undermine the remaining Social-Democratic and Rooseveltian factions that existed in the late 1980s. Bill Clinton signed the widely unpopular North American Free Trade Agreement (NAFTA).

In the aftermath of de-industrialization, which escalated under Bill Clinton's presidency, some regions of the United States are experiencing things similar to what took place in Russia during the 1990s. Factories have closed their doors, with the stable employment and high wages they symbolized being eliminated. Heroin addiction and suicide rates across the United States are the highest they have been in decades.

Donald Trump's campaign has made a point of reaching out to those who have been highly affected by de-industrialization in places like Ohio, Michigan, Pennsylvania, and Wisconsin. According to left-wing Film-maker Michael Moore: "Trump is going to hammer Clinton on this and her support of TPP and other trade policies that have royally screwed the people of these four states."

Hillary Rodham Clinton, as the first lady of President Bill Clinton, and Secretary of State during the first years of the Obama administration, is associated with the swift imposition of globalist capitalism and the deregulation of markets.

As Secretary of State, Clinton directed NATO's destruction of Libya. Libya once had an Islamic Socialist government that was centered around publicly owned oil resources. Libya had the highest life expectancy on the African continent. Like her husband's efforts to dismantle the Soviet system in Russia, Clinton's toppling of "Islamic Socialism" and imposition of "Free Markets" have been disastrous for Libya. The conditions in Libya have gotten so bad since the 2011 intervention that thousands of people have drowned, fleeing the country on rafts, hoping to cross the Mediterranean and reach Europe.

In the minds of many people across the planet, Hillary Clinton stands for free market policies, imposed by globalist banking institutions based in western countries. These policies have arguably resulted in an extreme amount of societal decay, and won Clinton many enemies.

When discussing the prospects of Hillary Clinton re-entering the White House, and how this is perceived across the planet, including Russia, this factor cannot be ignored.

CLINTON'S CAMPAIGN &
THE ROOTS OF CULTURAL LEFTISM

August 21st, 2016 - New Eastern Outlook

In recent speeches, including her speech accepting the Democratic Party's nomination for the Presidency, former Secretary of State Hillary Rodham Clinton has declared she would work to eradicate "systemic racism." Clinton did not present any specific strategy or policy to do this, yet each time she has uttered the two word phrase "systemic racism" there is a large burst of applause from her audience. An article from vox.com claimed that use of this term was "major" because it is a phrase that is "embraced in particular by younger activists."

In her speech, Clinton could have said she would work to eradicate "discrimination" or "underrepresentation" of minorities, but instead chose to use the favored buzzword of a specific political milieu to whom Clinton's campaign seems to be pandering. The phrase is part of a whole vocabulary of what some call "oppression theory." Young people have learned it from their University professors, namely those who teach Black or Gender Studies. This new lingo is used on various internet forums, especially Tumblr. When the Democratic Nomination was still up for grabs, the internet was filled with Clinton supporters who referred to Sanders supporters as "Bernie Bros", arguing that supporting the Presidential campaign of the Senator from Vermont was an expression of "white male privilege."

Blogs, tweets, and statuses now urge disappointed Sanders supporters to "check their privilege", consider ramifications of a Trump presidency, and vote for a candidate they despise. If a male Sanders supporter responds to these arguments and defends his decision to support Jill Stein or Gloria La Riva, or any candidate other than Clinton, he is accused of "man-splaining." As the argument continues, if an opponent of Clinton objects to a personal insult directed toward him, he is "tone-policing."

Where do these phrases come from? What is this political milieu that the Democratic Nominee has attached herself to? In the public eye it is often identified as the "far left." This is not completely accurate.

The entity known as the political left can trace its roots to the French Revolution of the 1790s. Since that time, people who identify as "leftists," revolutionaries, or radicals have used phrases like "liberty" and "solidarity," they have talked about working toward "emancipation" and "liberation" against "oppression." They have often used specifically Marxian formulations like "exploitation" and "expropriation" while advocating "power to the working class." With rhetoric about liberation and opposing injustice, the left has been the traditional home for opponents of racism, sexism, and advocates of social equality.

However, this new milieu that talks of "interconnectedness" and "intersectionality" rather than solidarity, and celebrates global military interventions done for "humanitarian" reasons, while engaging in heated debates about concepts like "cisgender privilege," accusing its detractors of being "white-splaining" "Bernie bros" who need to "check their privilege" is a new development, that did not arise naturally from within the left milieu.

The Congress for Cultural Freedom

To understand the unique rhetorical style that Clinton has embraced, one must understand what happened at the Waldorf-Astoria Hotel back in 1949. Despite the United States being in an anti-communist frenzy, with the House Un-American Activities committee in full swing, and many Communist Party members being sent to federal or state prisons, the Moscow-aligned Communist Party scored a key public relations victory.

On March 25th, 1949 the "Scientific and Cultural Conference for World Peace" opened in New York City, and gave voice to a loud, solid critique of US foreign policy. Albert Einstein, Will Geer, Arthur Miller, Aaron Copeland, Lillian Hellman, Frank Oppenheimer, Paul Robeson, W.E.B. Dubois, and many of the most well respected cultural and intellectual figures of the time took the stage at the conference.

The speeches not only denounced the military build-up against the Soviet Union, but also defended Soviet military interventions, and presented the USSR as a friendly, socialist society, not the "Iron Curtain" or "Evil Empire" portrayed in US media. The US Central Intelligence Agency watched with anger as images of the Waldorf Peace Conference were distributed by media outlets across the planet, discrediting the United States and raising the prestige of the Soviet Union.

In response, the following year the CIA launched a project called the "Congress for Cultural Freedom." Still today, the project is considered to be one of the agency's greatest achievements of the Cold War era. The CIA brags about the project on its website saying it involved: "a cadre of energetic and well-connected staffers willing to experiment with unorthodox ideas and controversial individuals if that was what it took to challenge the Communists at their own game."

The project involved indirect CIA funding of "cultural leftism." Across the United States and western Europe, Socialists, Communists, Anarchists, as well as artists, musicians, academics and film-makers started getting CIA money. Many of them were unaware of where this money came from.

The CIA's website confirms that it subsidized the New York-based Trotskyist magazine called "Partisan Review." The magazine presented itself as representing the genuine socialism of Karl Marx, Max Shachtman and Leon Trotsky, while opposing "Stalinism" in the USSR. The CIA also promoted the works of Sidney Hook and other "socialist" college professors.

The anti-Soviet "socialist" academic Sidney Hook was hired by the CIA as part of its "Congress for Cultural Freedom" program which began in 1950.

The project went beyond just political activism, and included funding for art galleries, experimental film-makers, and most especially, left-wing academics. The CIA funded the printing of George Orwell's writings, as well as concerts by left-wing musicians. A 2014 article from the Chronicle of Higher Education bemoans the impact of CIA funding for the Iowa Writers Workshop, which promoted what was described as stylistic innovations and breakthroughs in literature.

Why Foment "Cultural Leftism?"

It seems strange that at the time of the Cold War, the US government was intentionally funding people who called themselves radical leftists. However, it makes sense for one key reason: all of the artists, activists, academics, and philosophers who received money from the CIA program were staunchly anti-Soviet.

The CIA intentionally promoted "cultural leftists" hoping to divert people with leftist and dissident instincts away from Soviet Communism. A significant political gap between western leftists and the USSR was already developing. Over the course of the 1920s, the Soviet Union grew to be much more socially conservative than during its earliest years. Homosexuality and abortion were outlawed, and the state awarded medals to women who bore more than 10 children.

While western leftists clung to abstract Marxist concepts like "free love" and "the destruction of gender," the Soviet Union, fighting for its survival amidst blockades, invasions and foreign subversion, needed to tighten up. Facing constant attack, the Soviet Union was forced to become very authoritarian. With its industries rapidly developing within a previously poor and agrarian society, the Soviet economy required strict regulation. As they faced foreign attacks, Soviet leaders invoked not only Marxist-Leninist principles, but also Russian nationalism. Films portrayed medieval Czars not as tyrants but as patriotic idols fighting off foreign invaders. During the Second World War the Russian Orthodox Church was resurrected and allowed to function within Soviet society.

Despite having a centrally planned, non-capitalist economy, achieving what was often described as "economic miracles" by economists, when it came to cultural issues, the USSR simply did not live up to fantasies of many western leftists. Many activists who strove for an egalitarian paradise with "total freedom" were quite disappointed with what the Soviet Union had become.

Yet, even despite the growing divide, the Soviet Union had a huge network of international allies. The Communist International and broader People's Front of anti-fascists represented a massive global current. After the Second World War, the current got even larger around the world due to the very admirable role played by Communists and the USSR itself during the war. Starting in 1950 the CIA began working to exploit and expand the gap between western radicals and the Soviet Union, in the hope of isolating and defeating the USSR. From the earliest days, some of the project's participants were already fantasizing about events similar to the "color revolutions" the CIA would be involved in a few decades later. When the project was being planned, the ex-Communist academic Sidney Hook said: "Give me a hundred million dollars and a thousand dedicated people, and I will guarantee to generate such a wave of democratic unrest among the masses—yes, even among the soldiers—of Stalin's own empire, that all his problems for a long period of time to come will be internal. I can find the people."

Regardless of their intentions, in funding and promoting "Cultural Leftism" the CIA ultimately remolded the left-wing of politics in the USA and Western Europe.

Eastern Mysticism, Fascism & The Occult

In Western Europe and the United States, Christianity represented the most prominent religious perspective and was promoted by the most centrist and mainstream elements of the political establishment. The radical left generally promoted philosophical materialism and scientific atheism. The occult, paganism, and eastern mysticism were an obsession of the extreme right.

The Nazis, who considered themselves to be a "party of the right" had glorified Germany's pre-Christian religions, frequently invoking Oden and Valhalla in their propaganda. The famed Occultist Aleister Crowley who entertained the rich and powerful in Britain often vocally aligned with the

The German Nazis and Italian fascists embraced the Dalai Lama's primitive authoriarian regime in Tibet.

Conservative Party and considered leftists to be a dirty crowd of uncultured rabble rousers. As a staunch right-winger the iconic para-normalist said "I hate Christianity as socialists hate soap."

European fascists often marveled at India's caste system, seeing it as an antidote to class struggle. Julius Evola, one of the primary Italian far-right intellectuals was also considered an expert on Hinduism and pre-Christian mythology. The Nazis adopted the Swastika as their emblem and called themselves "Aryans" because they identified themselves with the authoritarian structures of ancient India, and believed Germans to genetic descendants of it.

Within India, the caste system, mystical practices that are designed to attract spirits, along with the strict patriarchal family structure have been the main targets of social reformers. Many leftists in India accused the British empire of working to reinforce these things in order to effectively weaken the struggle for independence.

Regardless of left and right norms, following the 1950s, as the "Cultural Left" was re-energized while being re-molded by CIA funding in the United States, it was filled with admirers of traditional Indian culture. Writers like Jack Kerouac and Allen Ginsberg used Hindu chants in their writings, which were distributed and promoted at Universities. The International Society for Krishna Consciousness, a very conservative and anti-communist sect that worships a Hindu Diety became iconic participants in peace marches.

Similarly, the theocratic and feudal kingdom of Tibet was rewritten into a trendy liberal cause. The Dalai Lama's regime was considered to be one of the most right-wing, authoritarian and patriarchal kingdoms in the world. The Nazis had been so impressed with the harshly enforced traditional structures of the Kingdom, that they had dispatched many delegations to study it. The Nazis had actively worked with the regime to fight the Nationalist and Communist forces in other parts of China.

In the 1950s, the CIA sponsored a campaign of guerrilla warfare intended to drive the Communist Party of China from the Tibet Autonomous Region and restore feudal theocratic rule. The book "The CIA's Secret War in Tibet", published by the Heritage Foundation, tells how the Dalai Lama's brother led a team of violent insurgents who were airdropped into Tibet with US made weapons.

However, the remolded Cultural Left which Hillary Clinton now embraces, nearly worships the Dalai Lama. The "Free Tibet" movement, which calls for breaking up the People's Republic of China, is now one of the trendiest "left-wing" causes. One of the favorite books of this "movement" is "Seven Years in Tibet", written by Heinrich Harrier, a member of Hitler's SS, who had been dispatched to Tibet during the Second World War.

"Tune in, Turn On, Drop Out"

The political left had long been outspoken opponents of recreational drug use. Many of the early socialists even opposed drinking alcohol and were part of the broader temperance movement of the early 20th century. However, as CIA money flowed in, forging the anti-Soviet "cultural left" this position was also altered.

According to what was revealed by the Church Committee, a commission set up by the US Congress to investigate the CIA in 1975, the CIA had actively distributed drugs to college students and others as part of "Project MKULTRA." The CIA had involved many professors and academics in its research and distribution of Lysergic acid diethylamide (LSD) also called "acid."
This hallucinogen had first been synthetically created by Albert Hoffman, a Swiss chemist, in 1938. During the 1950s, the US Central Intelligence Agency had widely experimented with LSD, hoping it could be weaponized and used against the Soviet Union.

Timothy Leary, a Harvard psychology professor, became one of the most well known figures among left-wing students during the 1960s and 70s. He preached "tune in, turn on, and drop out" and loudly encouraged young people who opposed the Vietnam War and racism to use LSD. In 1999, FBI files were released showing that Dr. Timothy Leary had been an FBI informant for much his career.

As the cultural left emerged, there was a strange re-orientation of the mainstream US media. The press backed away from hard line celebrations of capitalism and condemnations of dissent. Instead a large section of popular rock bands, University professors, and TV programs almost celebrated the "New Left," specifically its cultural manifestations.

During the upsurge of left-wing political activism during the 1960s and 70s, many Communists who took political direction from the Soviet Union, China, or Cuba identified the campus based, drug using, promiscuous, and well funded anti-Soviet "New Left" as problematic. These forces that were organized into disciplined cadre organizations, were a minority, often labelled "Tankies" and "Hardliners" and denounced by iconic New Left figures like Jerry Rubin.

By the mid-1970s, the New Left's political strength had died down. It remained a kind of small "loyal opposition" in US politics. Peace marches took place, the Green Party was formed, and the New Left functioned as a place that could absorb free thinkers and others with grievances against US society.

While the New Left remained isolated, the US government was ruled by people who espoused Neo-Con formulations about "the greatest country in the world" and called capitalism "the greatest system ever created." The Ford Foundation, various Rockefeller think tanks, along with projects directed by George Soros funneled money to many who would be considered "left of center," but they remained a small bloc that was ignored by major political forces.

The New Left Takes Power

The turning point came after the failures of the Bush administration and the 2008 financial crisis dramatically changed the political atmosphere. The USA clearly has big problems now, and the Republican Party's political message of "my country right or wrong" and "don't fix it if it ain't broke" would no longer suffice.

Amidst Republican confusion and re-messaging, the Democratic Party has now emerged as the most powerful entity in US politics. In order to maintain its grip on power, the Obama presidency and the Clinton campaign are re-energizing the "Cultural Left."

In 2016, the foot soldiers of the Democratic Party are those who have been trained in NGO funded, University based Cultural Leftism. With the global Communist movement far weaker now, the remnants and descendants of the CIA's "New Left" have a high level of ideological dominance. What was once considered "counter-culture" has become the mainstream.

Now that opponents of the United States on the global stage are much more socially conservative, the pro-war and imperialistic message of the Cultural Left is far more pronounced. At times,

Hillary Clinton's campaign against Donald Trump sounds almost conservative. The Clinton campaign insinuates that Trump is unpatriotic for avoiding military service during the Vietnam War, and unqualified for the Presidency because he uses "offensive" language. According to Clinton's supporters, Trump is loyal to the Kremlin and admires "dictators" i.e. regimes that challenge Wall Street dominance.

Hillary Clinton thundered "America is great, because America is good" during her convention speech, dismissing Trump's "Make America Great Again" as unpatriotic. Many of the attacks leveled against Trump are not condemning him for being bigoted or authoritarian, but rather for being overcritical of US society and embracing "conspiracy theories."

According to politics extolled by the Clinton-ites and their foot soldiers, being left-wing, fighting for women's rights, and opposing injustice means carrying out regime change. According to Clinton's Cultural Left, the battle for "human rights" must continue, and the Pentagon must be utilized to free women, homosexuals, transgender people, and others from "dictators" who do not share their enlightened social perspective. This liberation is to be carried out by arming Islamic extremists, enacting economic sanctions, and firing cruise missiles in order to create chaos and topple regimes deemed to be promoting values contrary to those taught in Race and Gender Studies courses.

Greater confrontation with Russia is considered a good thing because its government is accused of being "homophobic." Those who point out that Clinton coddles dictators in places like Saudi Arabia, or that US meddling in Syria and Libya has strengthened the menace of ISIL are labelled "conspiracy theorists" who need to "check their privilege" and "stop man-splaining."

At the same time, pointing out that the US backed anti-government fighters in Syria are actually Wahabbi fanatics who have slaughtered Christians and Alawites is called "Islamophobia." Consistent with the argumentative style of the campus based "privilege politics" milieu, these facts are never refuted. Rather, one is simply accused of some ideological crime or impurity for pointing them out.

As millions of people are rapidly fleeing both Libya and Syria because NATO interventions have toppled independent nationalist governments and made their lives unlivable, leftists are applauding the situation. Rather than protest these imperialist crimes which created a mass refugee crisis, the bulk of leftists are having parades to "Welcome the Refugees." Those who point out that NATO destabilizations have caused a crisis of mass migration, and say this is an atrocity that should be opposed, are accused of being bigots and Islamophobes.

The Growing Danger of War

The left that existed prior to the Second World War is something that Clinton-ites would never recognize. Books like "Toward Soviet America" by William Z. Foster in 1932 laid out a blue print for a planned economy in the United States, and called for hungry, unemployed working class people in Kentucky, Ohio, Alabama, and elsewhere to fight back and demand better working conditions.

The mass movements of the 1930s won the creation of social security, unemployment insurance, veterans benefits, and much more. The slogan the Communist Party used was "Don't Starve, Fight!" Those who were mobilized were not an well educated cultural elite, but industrial workers, unemployed youth, students, and all kinds of other ordinary Americans who were suffering during the economic crisis known as the Great Depression.

The manufactured and recently empowered "cultural left" with which Clinton has aligned herself would look at such people and tell them they deserve to be destitute, because it would help them better understand what people of color have experienced. It would tell them that demanding jobs was a sense of "entitlement" and "white privilege." It would tell them that they should celebrate the prospects of war with Russia or China because it would be mean toppling leaders portrayed to be "homophobic" or "oppressive of women."

Now that the "left" has become something miles away from what it once was, it should be no surprise that lots of working class white people are embracing Donald Trump and the "alternative right." Many white people who are suffering during the economic downturn have come to see the left as a current that seeks to punish and shame them, not improve their living situation. Furthermore, the modern left is perceived as looking down on them for not knowing the appropriate "oppression theory" lingo which is being taught at Universities.

Prior to the Second World War, the United States had a vast, working class, anti-capitalist movement.

If organizations emerged that actually made economic appeals, and organized against big money interests, in a way that is similar to what was done during the 1930s, the situation could be drastically altered.

However, that is not the case. The "new left," specifically fostered to counter the influence of global opponents of western capitalism, has now taken the helm of western civilization, staffed with a cadre of loyal crusaders fighting in the name of "diversity" and "intersectionality." Meanwhile, the economy is getting worse and the danger of a bigger military clash between the United States and Russia or China, the two largest countries on earth, is rapidly growing.

Part Two: Trump & Populism

IMMIGRATION, "PEASANT CULTURES" & THE NEW RIGHT-WING NATIONALISM

January 12th, 2017 - New Eastern Outlook

Global media is abuzz with talk of the "New Nationalism" that is sweeping the western world. US media talks specifically of the "Alt Right." So, why is it that figures like Marine Le Pen, Donald Trump, Steve Bannon and Nigel Farrage are on the rise? In a desperate attempt to explain it, some analysts have gone as far as to say that the new political shift is due to some sort of Russian conspiracy. The reason for the revival of right-wing populism and authoritarianism is in fact rooted in a deeper reality currently plaguing western politics.

Two well-known American pundits, Cenk Uygur and Ann Coulter, recently sat down for a debate at a conference called "Politicon" in Los Angeles. The exchange got heated as the two barbed back and forth about a variety of political issues.

Ann Coulter, the right-wing analyst who is also the daughter of the anti-Communist witch-hunter Jack Coulter, did her best to focus the conversation on the issue of immigration, which is part of her recent political makeover. Coulter's career began during the late years of Clinton, and escalated under the Bush administration. The books that defined her career, with titles like "Slander", "Treason" and "How to Talk to a Liberal" were neoconservative defenses of aggressive US foreign policy and free market capitalism. In the picture her earlier works painted of the United States, those who faced economic hardship were a bunch of lazy whiners who needed to go out and get a job, while US foreign policy was a benevolent form of international charity in which the Pentagon selflessly liberated people being oppressed by dictators and terrorists.

Coulter has had to re-invent herself in recent years. The base of the Republican Party, the suburban and rural white American working class, are no longer economically prosperous. They are increasingly isolationist in their views and do not approve of continued US meddling around the globe. With her nose to the ground, Coulter has shifted from the neocon narrative, in which America is perfect and dissidents are traitors, and has slowly evolved into a nationalist and right-wing populist along the lines of Britain's Nigel Farrage.

The New Right & The Global Crisis

During the debate, Coulter went on a tirade against immigrants from both the Middle East and Latin America. She said "It's simply a fact: we are bringing in peasant cultures." She cited the fact that many Middle Eastern countries have primitive, medieval style legal systems. She cited the fact that many of the immigrant children from Central America had never seen a flushing toilet before.

The response of Cenk Uygur and his liberal audience was to boo and accuse Coulter of being "racist" and "bigoted." Aside from holding her feet to the fire regarding her statements about nuclear weapons, Uygurs response was not very persuasive, especially to those within Coulter's right-wing fan base. Those who admire Ann Coulter and voted for Donald Trump are impressed with the boldness of those who are "not politically correct" and break taboos of politeness and cultural sensitivity.

The facts that Coulter cited were in many ways accurate. Saudi Arabia, Qatar, Bahrain, Jordan, UAE and Oman do indeed have primitive legal systems. Many impoverished people in Central and

South America do not have access to running to water. Criminal gangs plague Latin America, and terrorist and extremist groups like Al-Queda, ISIS or the Muslim Brotherhood have a lot of influence in the Middle East. All of this is true, though Coulter points it out in a rather crass and insensitive way.

The reality is that millions of people throughout the world, not only in Latin America and the Middle East, but also in Southeast Asia, the islands of the pacific, and many other places, simply cannot live in their homelands any longer, and are fleeing in big numbers. The occurrence is widely recognized as a global crisis of mass migration.

The liberals of Cenk Uygur's ilk, and even some of the hard left "socialists" and "communists" celebrate mass migration like it is somehow a good thing. They talk about "the American dream" of "coming to a new land." They shout slogans like "no one is illegal" and "we are all immigrants" with a big smile on their faces. While the political left rightly opposes bigotry and any further repression of immigrant workers, in the process, they ignore a very real humanitarian catastrophe which is shaking the planet. Corpses are discovered on a daily basis on the US border with Mexico. Many migrants have died attempting to cross the Mediterranean to Europe.

It should be no surprise that many working class people in the United States and Europe, who directly observe this inflow of impoverished workers, see a rise in violence, and are increasingly afraid of being killed in terrorist attacks, are rallying behind right-wingers like Trump, Farrage, and Coulter, who at least acknowledge that the problem exists, and claim to offer solutions to it.

Wall Street Oil Bankers & Primitive Regimes

The reason that anti-immigration politicians and activists are often called "racist" is because much of their rhetoric insinuates that those from foreign lands who travel to the west are inherently criminal, dirty, violent or somehow inferior to the westerners. This belief that some peoples are just naturally inferior to others is the textbook definition of racism. Though this kind of blatant racism was widely promoted and accepted by western capitalist powers at one time, it has now become largely unacceptable in public discourse, mainly as a result of the political upheavals which took place the 1960s and 70s.

If one can reject notions of racial supremacy, certain facts must still be addressed surrounding the issue of immigration and cultural diversity.

"Peasant Cultures," the derogatory and disrespectful phrase used by Ann Coulter is not completely off the mark when describing the legal

The Wahabbi autocracy in Saudi Arabia is one of the only countries in the world currently utilizing public beheading as a method of execution.

systems of certain parts of the Middle East. Saudi Arabia is certainly a "peasant culture," or more accurately a "Bedouin culture." The ruling elite still live in tents, and Saudi women are not legally permitted to drive cars. People are routinely beheaded and crucified for crimes like "sorcery" or "insulting the King." More than 30% of the population are foreign born "guest workers," who exist essentially as slaves. The setup of Saudi society is indeed barbarism, and many within Saudi Arabia, especially Shia Muslim oil workers who endure the horrors of this backward system on a daily basis, are the first to point this out.

Those who would attempt to dismiss the horrific, repressive nature of Saudi society as merely "a different culture" or a "different way of life" are completely disingenuous and should not be taken seriously. However, Saudi Arabia is not the natural outgrowth of Arab civilization. The borders of the Arab world were drawn in the Sykes-Picot Agreement, a secret treaty among western powers.

The House of Saud was selected and propped up by the British empire for geo-strategic reasons. In the 1940s, the Saudi Royal Family became fast friends of America's financial elite. The Wall Street monopolists of Exxon-Mobile, many major politicians of both the Democratic and Republican Parties, are deeply tied to the Saudi regime. Saudi Arabia sells oil to American oil giants, and purchases a huge number of weapons from Pentagon contractors. Ronald Reagan's administration made clear in 1981 that it would send troops to protect the regime "if there should be anything that resembled an internal revolution in Saudi Arabia."

Like Saudi Arabia, the primitive regimes that repress women, torture, behead, and have absolutist monarchs across the Middle East region, are close allies of the United States government and the financial western monopolists. They sell oil to western corporations, and purchase weapons from US military contractors. Almost all of these regimes, be it Kuwait, Bahrain, or United Arab Emirates; nearly all of these primitive, barbaric monarchies are deeply involved in NATO backed efforts to topple the Syrian government. They also echo in Israeli officials fiery denunciations of the Islamic Republic of Iran as being somehow a threat to world peace.

Targeting the Modernizers, Halting Development

While the most savage and backward autocracies have been propped up by the USA, what regimes are targeted by the Pentagon and NATO? Iraq was led by the Baath Arab Socialist Party. Saddam Hussein was a secular leader, who vastly improved the conditions of women in his country, and also modernized and industrialized Iraq. The US invaded Iraq, destroyed the country's infrastructure, and hung Saddam Hussein. What was once a stable, independent economy that was gradually becoming more modern and civilized, has been reduced to chaos.

The Syrian Arab Republic, currently in the crosshairs of the Pentagon and US funded "regime change" operations, is yet another independent, nationalist government. The Syrian Baathist government has worked with Russia and China to industrialize the country and bring in infrastructure, while at the same time modernizing the society. In Syria, Christians, Alawites, Druze, and Sunnis have lived together in peace for decades. Women in Syria have full constitutional equality. Many Syrian industrial workers are organized into unions that exercise collective bargaining power. Syria, unlike its Wall Street friendly Arab neighbors, is not a "peasant culture" but an impoverished country in a strategic region, led by independent patriotic forces that are desperately trying to modernize and develop.

After the Islamic Revolution of 1979, the leader of the revolution, Ayatollah Khomeni called forth a "construction Jihad." Iranians were mobilized to build highways, airports, and other infrastructure. Unlike all the Emirates, Kingdoms, and US backed oil autocracies, Iran has contested elections in which "hardliners" and "moderates" compete for elected office. In Iran, the majority of those

The "Bridge of Nature" in Northern Tehran is a shining example of infrastructure development carried out since Iran's 1979 anti-capitalist revolution.

attending public universities are women. University education and healthcare is free to all citizens, and the society is tightly organized with the Basij organizations volunteering and enforcing the revolution on a local level.

US media fixates on portraying Bashar Assad as a dictator. They claim Syria's elections are illegitimate, and that the ruling Baath Arab Socialist Party is corrupt. However, the King of Saudi Arabia makes no pretense of being democratically elected. Neither does the King of Jordan, the King of Bahrain, or those who rule Kuwait, the United Arab Emirates, and other US aligned regimes in the region. Syria does not conduct public floggings or beheading. Syria allows religious diversity.

Criticism of Iran and Syria can most certainly be made, but compared to the autocratic oil monarchies who are aligned with Wall Street and the Pentagon, they are very advanced in terms of human rights, the rule of law, and basic societal health. The Islamic REPUBLIC of Iran and the Syrian Arab REPUBLIC exist as "Republics" in a region full of Kingdoms, Emirates and Sultans who openly behead, torture, and deny basic human rights to their people. Yet it is these independent regimes, republics, with elections and leaders who pursue modernization that are targeted by the western capitalist powers and their allies, who simultaneously prop up and align with the most barbaric "peasant cultures."

Furthermore, while liberals insist on being "politically correct" and just shout "Islamophobe" at anyone who dares say it, in addition to political backwardness, another issue that plagues the Middle East region is terrorism and violent extremism. But why is terrorism so prevalent in the Middle East?

The ideology embraced by ISIS, Al-Queda, Al-Nusra, and almost every other murderous terrorist organization in the Arab world is an extremist distortion of Sunni Islam called "Wahabbism." Wahabbism is the state ideology, not of Iran or Syria, but of Saudi Arabia. Osama Bin Laden, said to be the mastermind behind the 9/11 attacks, comes from one of the most wealthy families in Saudi Arabia. The multi-billionaire Bin Laden family has a state enforced monopoly on construction within the Kingdom, and is extremely well connected. The previously redacted 28 pages of the 9/11 commission report, reveal all kinds of links between the government of Saudi Arabia, and Wahabbi terrorism.

Bahrain, Kuwait, the United Arab Emirates and the Hashemite Kingdom of Jordan are deeply involved in cooperating with Wahabbi terrorists and fanatics, some of whom are linked to Al-Queda, in an effort to topple the Syrian government. The majority of the hijackers who carried the 9/11 attacks were openly identified as being Saudi citizens.

Who Supports The Terrorists & Drug Dealers?

Barbaric, murderous terrorist groups certainly exist in the Arab world. However, these groups are linked to US backed regimes, and have been utilized by western countries to attack the independent states which are desperately trying to modernize. Starting in 1979, the USA spent over a decade funding Wahabbi terrorist groups as they fought to topple the secular People's Democratic Party in Afghanistan. The United States currently cooperates with such organizations in its efforts to topple the Syrian government.

The political left mostly refuses to acknowledge the Wahabbi terrorism is a real problem in the Middle East. It screams about "Islamophobia" and holds parades to "welcome the refugees." It cheers for the "Syrian Revolution" led by Wahabbi terrorists. When the right-wing makes bigoted, ignorant statements about the Arab peoples, or those who practice the Islamic faith, the left's only response is a kind of semantic scolding. They scold the right for breaking taboos and saying certain things, but do not dig into the reality of the region or its history. This shrill tone and lack of any real depth or analysis allows the crass right-wing to create a racist caricature of all Muslims, Persians, and Arabs. The right-wing looks like it is being "bold" by acknowledging what the left refuses to permit any discussion of.

The same can be said for Latin America. Guatemala, Honduras, and Mexico are a mess of poverty and criminal violence. Central American countries hold the world's top murder rates. South of the US border, drug cartels and other criminal organizations engage in horrendous crimes that are horrifying to any rational person. These thugs and murderers operate near the US border, on both sides, and do horrendous things. Their activities have intensified in recent years, and the areas of the United States near the southern border have not been immune to their violence.

Pointing out this reality is not "racist" as the cowardly, non-ideological left screams at all who point it out. The victims of these monstrous criminals are primarily other people of Central American and Latino backgrounds, and they are the first to denounce these crimes, and point out the crisis. A wave of vigilante anti-drug groups have formed across Mexico to fight the drug cartels.But what is the roots of the drug related violence and chaos in this region?

The infamous "School of the Americas" in the US State of Georgia trained many murderous thugs in the art of torture, assassination, and war crimes.

Many of the "contras" funded by the United States in Nicaragua, and paramilitary groups propped in Colombia, were directly involved in the drug trade during the 1980s.

Even today, the majority of the weapons used by the drug cartels in Mexico originate in the United States. Drug cartels in Mexico have, not only the kind of hunting rifles and hand guns that can be legally purchased in the USA, but also military grade assault rifles and other equipment that was somehow acquired from the US military. The United States trains the Mexican police forces and supplies them with weapons, when they have a reputation for being completely corrupt and bought off by the drug cartels in many areas.Guatemala has endured decades of violence. The roots of this chaos goes back to when the United States supported violent paramilitaries who slaughtered the indigenous peoples throughout the 1970s and 80s.

Honduras elected a socialist President, Manuel Zelaya who wanted to stabilize the country and sought independent economic development. The United States supported the military in toppling him in 2009 with a brutal military coup d'etat. Hillary Clinton discussed her support for the Honduran coup in her book "Hard Choices." Since the independent socialist President Manuel Zelaya was overthrown, Honduras has been a mess of crime and poverty, and though the recent statistics are quibbled about, it is often listed as "murder capital of the world."

The new western right would like to present peoples of Latin-American decent as inherently criminal and inferior. The political left simply screams "racist" at anyone who dares point out the reality of poverty and criminal violence in the region. What is ignored is that the real problem of gang and drug violence in Central and South America is a result of international bankers trying to hold back development and secure a monopoly for themselves.

While Mexico, Guatemala, and Honduras are a mess of violence, Nicaragua is a bastion of stability in Central America. The Sandinista government, which is routinely decried as a "dictatorship" in American media, has drastically reduced poverty, provided housing and education to the population. Just like in the Middle East, it is the independent, nationalist governments, like Nicaragua, Venezuela, Bolivia, and Ecuador that are targets of US intervention and destabilization. Like Wahabbi terrorism in the Middle East, the drug related violence and instability in Central and South America is something that has been imposed on Latin America.

The funding of paramilitaries and drug linked criminal organizations was part of US efforts in the 1980s to topple various Marxist governments in the region. While independent nationalist governments like the Sandinistas have tried to develop, build infrastructure, and modernize their countries, it is the west that has unleashed drugs and violence in an effort to hold back development.

Impoverishing, Not Developing The World

Why is it that children from so many countries around the world have never seen a flushing toilet? Is it because they are inherently "dirty" or inferior peoples as Coulter would have us believe? No. It is because Wall Street monopolists and bankers have held back development.

Nigeria is the top oil exporting country on the African continent. The oil rich Niger Delta Region is home to some of the most impoverished peoples on the planet. Photographs show the horrendous and primitive conditions lived in by these people. The ground the beaches they play on are often stained black with oil. Western corporations like British Petroleum and Royal Dutch Shell have made countless billions from the Niger Delta, but the people there live in extreme poverty.

Nigeria, the top oil exporting country in Africa is now facing a massive crisis of malnutrition according to the world food program.

Libya was once the top oil producing country on the African continent. The Islamic Socialist government of Moammar Gaddafi created Africa's most efficient water system. Free University education was provided, and Libyans had a lifestyle that the envy of almost everyone else on the continent. Women in Libya held important roles in local levels of the government. It was the USA and NATO that toppled this independent nationalist government. Now, Libyans are fleeing their home country as refugees. The formerly prosperous country has been completely wrecked. Poverty has been forcibly imposed on the people of what was once the most prosperous African country.

What is worse, is that the same kind of controlled economic demolition imposed on Libya, Central America, and the Middle East is now taking place, to a much milder degree, within the borders of the United States.

The new low wage economic order is devastating places like Michigan, Pennsylvania, Ohio, and Wisconsin, states that were key in securing Trump's victory. These places no longer have good paying industrial jobs, but instead have short term service sector employment. The rates of opiate overdoses, suicide, mental illness, crime and other societal ills spawned by a sudden drop in the standard of living are rising. In the last 8 years, the number of Americans applying for nutritional assistance has increased by 32%.

Silicon Valley, New York City, and some gentrified urban areas of the USA are seeing a new level of stability, but for the rustbelt it's a very different story. Millions of people in the economically devastated areas voted for Donald Trump because he acknowledged these problems, while Clinton spoke of Obama's presidency as being successful and promised more of the same.

Trump spoke about the suffering of millions of Americans. He blamed "international bankers" for wrecking the lives of America's working people. Trump even went as far as to acknowledge the negative results of US foreign policy in Iraq and Syria, where terrorism has been strengthened. Trump dared to condemn Saudi Arabia. His rhetoric embraced the rising isolationist sentiments, which have increased on both the left and the right.

The New Nationalists Fill A Void

Trump's right-wing nationalism filled a void among an entire strata of American society which is disgusted by the current conditions wrought by American capitalism. Due to the fact that the organized political left makes no solid appeal to the rustbelt working class, they are rallying behind Trump, who appeals to them as a savior. The crowds of protesters outside of Trump's rallies offered no explanation for why millions of refugees and immigrants are pouring into the western countries, or how the crisis could be stopped. Many of the left-wing activists who protested Trump have openly supported the "regime change" operations in Libya and Syria which have unleashed terrorism and a wave of refugees into Europe. The only message the left has offered the Trump supporters is a nasty rebuke of "racist!"

The surprise victory of Donald Trump was not because millions of Americans were impressed with his program or proposed solutions. Trump's proposals were rather fluid and inconsistent. Other than his plan for a big wall between the USA and Mexico, and to "bring back the jobs" he statements were often quite vague. Some of Trump's economic agenda seemed populist and social-democratic, other parts of it seemed free market and neoliberal. Trump did emphasize support for policing agencies, and seemed to play into a disgust at "Black Lives Matter" protests among white Americans who sympathize with the police.

The rise of Trump, as well as the rise of various right-wing populist currents across western Europe is not the result of a Russian conspiracy. It is also not indicative of a pending mass genocide or the creation of a new Third Reich, as certain alarmist voices claim. The situation is this: Nations, countries, and communities all over the world are being impoverished and thrown into chaos by global capitalism. Working people's lives are being destroyed in both the first and third worlds.

Stability is one of the most basic human needs. People need to feel in touch with the world around them. The lives of people in the western world once involved a higher level of stability and security than any other peoples in the world, but this has been swept away. The day to day insecurity and fears associated with short term, low wage employment, as well as the increased presence and over site of government surveillance and policing agencies is drastically changing the lifestyle of people in western countries.

Multiculturalism is causing an increasing amount of ideological insecurity and confusion, with many becoming increasing unsure of what is right and wrong, and looking desperately for purpose in their lives. This is all compounded by the fear of terrorism and crime, which is visibly increasing. The political left allows no real discussion of these issues, and sticks to abstract slogans against "racism."

To millions of people in the west, the left has become synonymous with the political establishment, which holds no answer to the crisis.

To millions, "socialism" is no longer a call for a new political system in which society controls and plans the economy, but instead has become a euphemism for expanding social welfare programs. Many confused Americans will say things like "the USA is half socialist already."

The left exists in a kind of "movementist" vacuum where slogans and protest chants take the place of substantive analysis or proposals. The left does not explain that mass migration, drug gangs and Wahabbi terrorism is caused by the international financial order. The left does not offer radical proposals about how improve the lives of working people in the western countries. The left does not expose the criminal nature of US foreign policy, and often cheers on State Department "revolutions" across the planet. While the far-right embraces a bombastic and radical sounding tone filled with anger and demanding change, leftist political rallies often sound like a kind of group therapy involving "safe spaces" and "self-care."

As a result the newly remolded right-wing, which offers a watered down version of 20th century right-wing nationalism and populism, is providing a worldview and program for moving forward. The far-right is stepping up to the plate, giving voice to peoples anger, as bigoted as it may be, and offering its own solutions, as flawed as they are.

In western political discourse, the far-right wing is almost the only radical sounding alternative to the status quo that delivers a coherent message, and acknowledges the problems that are radicalizing and politicizing people.

The new nationalist right-wing is in ascendancy for one reason: disaffected people who want solutions will only turn to those who actually claim to offer them.

CAN TRUMP REALLY
CLAIM THE LEGACY OF AMERICAN
POPULISM?

February 2nd, 2017 - Mint Press News

Donald Trump's ascendency to the White House
involved endless appeals to "the people" and
denunciations of the elite.

During an October rally, for example, Trump said:
"It's a global power structure that is responsible
for the economic decisions that have robbed our
working class, stripped our country of its wealth
and put that money into the pockets of a handful
of large corporations and political entities."

His inauguration speech was laced in similar
rhetoric:

During his Presidential campaign Donald Trump called for rebuilding the roads and infrastructure of the USA.

"The establishment protected itself, but not the citizens of our country. Their victories have not been your victories. Their triumphs have not been your triumphs. And while they celebrated in our nation's Capital, there was little to celebrate for struggling families all across our land. That all changes — starting right here and right now because this moment is your moment: it belongs to you."

Populism is defined as political rhetoric championing the common person, the working class, or the disenfranchised. While in the present period populism is associated with right-wing nationalism, the nature of populism has shifted and evolved throughout U.S. history. Right-wing populism in the 21st century is just the latest incarnation of a quite diverse trend.

'You are a worker"

"You are a worker," a widely read pamphlet begins.

"One nice morning you are told your services are no longer needed. In plain words: you are fired. You are thrown out. ... The employer has no more work for you. He cuts operations or he shuts his plant altogether. While you remain without a livelihood, he goes to his country estate or abroad to have a good time. ...

And yet, come to think of it, you are not a stranger to this factory or mill or shop. You and the like of you have built it. You and the like of you have created all the machinery, all the raw material and all the fuel which is necessary to run an industry. ... It is your blood, your sweat, your muscle and your brain that is sunk into every piece of goods produced.

You have much at stake in this establishment — your whole life. It is yours, more than the owner's. It is part of your very self. ...

Has it ever occurred to you that such a state of affairs is wrong?"

This isn't from a Donald Trump speech. This isn't from an alt-right rant against globalism. The above text comes from "Why Communism? Plain Talk on Vital Questions," published in 1933 by

Moissaye J. Olgin, a leader of the New York City branch of the Communist Party.

The Communist Party and the unemployed councils it directed involved hundreds of thousands of working class people, black and white, both native-born and immigrants. Together they stopped evictions. Later in the decade, they organized industrial unions in a wave of sit-down strikes.

With slogans like "Fight or Starve!" they pushed the Roosevelt administration to create many key reforms, such as Social Security, unemployment insurance, food assistance, and the Works Progress Administration.

Olgin and the Communist Party's methods of agitation were not new in 1933. A generation prior, the activist, union leader, and Socialist Party presidential candidate Eugene Debs had traveled the country on bright red train car, making similar arguments. Prior to the United States' entrance into World War I, the Socialist Party was a mass political formation that received over 900,000 votes — roughly 6 percent of the popular vote — in the 1912 presidential election.

Socialism: The original populism

However, the political discourse is quite different today. When I was in Wheeling, West Virginia in November, just after the election, I met a former steelworker, who preferred to remain anonymous. He told me how angry he was about the closing of steel mills and the deindustrialization of his hometown. He told me he had voted for Donald Trump because "the Democrats don't care about the working people anymore. Now they are a bunch of socialists."

The local United Steelworkers chapter apparently agreed. Local 2911 parted ways with the national leaders of the union and endorsed Trump.
An entire issue of Foreign Affairs, the publication of the Council on Foreign Relations, was dedicated to "The Power of Populism." The cover was donned with Grant Wood's famous "American Gothic" painting, showing a rural American couple, the husband clutching a pitchfork. The text of the publication describes a global confrontation between "populism" and the "open international system."

Extensive analysis of 1930s fascism is included, and an article on Latin America describes Chilean dictator Augusto Pinochet and Bolivian President

Evo Morales as "populists" and equates them with each other.

It is subtly sifting into the American consciousness that talk of the "working class" and "the common people" is inherently right wing. While talk of racism, sexism, and other forms of oppression or intolerance is associated with the political left, concerns about those who suffer on a class basis are now being labelled "right wing." Left-wing voices describe Trump supporters as "ignorant" and inform us that "educated" people are anti-racist. Meanwhile, observers say Trump is transforming Republicans into a "party of the working class."

The concept of the political left can trace its roots back to the French Revolution. The seating in the National Assembly was politically arranged, with the most radical sections sitting on the left side. "Leftism" emerged as a continent-wide current with the "spring of nations" in 1848.

Communism and socialism emerged as the most powerful ideological currents in a movement that encouraged the "working class" or the "proletariat" to rise up and overthrowing the "bourgeoisie," the owners of the banks and factories. Can any political ideology be more populist than this?

The political left saw racism, sexism, and national chauvinism as methods used by the rich to divide the working people and prevent them from rising up. While slogans like "workers of the world, unite!" were employed, the first communist seizure of power in 1871 was done under very nationalistic auspices. The workers of Paris saw the French state surrendering to foreign invaders. The Paris Commune was created as working class people waved the red, white, and blue flag and sought to defend the gains and ideals of the French Revolution from the Prussians.

The Leftist Origins of the Republican Party

The Republican Party certainly has populist roots, but this populism had a left-wing character. The very name "Republican" was taken from the various uprisings throughout Europe in the 1800s, in which "Republicanism" was the battle cry. The Republican Party emerged as the party of smaller farmers who opposed slavery, known as the "Free Soilers." It was also the party of religious abolitionists and labor unions. The slogan was, "Free Land, Free Labor, Free Men!"

In the 1860s, New York City's Republican Party-aligned newspaper was the New York Tribune, whose London correspondent was none other than the influential socialist thinker Karl Marx. August Willich and Joseph Wedemeyer, key leaders of the Union Army during the Civil War, served openly as members of Marx's International Workingmen's Association. In the 1864 presidential election, the global Marxist movement put its support behind Abraham Lincoln.

Following the Civil War, the "Radical Republicans" were considered the far left of American politics. They advocated racial equality and supported reconstruction. Republican President Ulysses S. Grant sent federal troops to fight the Ku Klux Klan, and even worked to restrict the atrocities against Native Americans in the western territories.

As the Republican Party moved away from the radical politics of its origins, what is commonly called the Populist movement emerged with the "People's Party" being formed during the 1890s. These were small-scale farmers, labor activists, feminists, and others who wanted to advance the fight for social equality. The Populists called for the nationalization of railroads, public control of banking, and other left-wing economic measures. Many populists condemned racism and lynching, while others openly embraced it.

The Populist upsurge included Henry George, known as a radical social reformer when he ran for mayor of New York in 1886. The Socialist Labor Party, led by Daniel De Leon, and eventually, the much larger Socialist Party of America, emerged from political upsurge. The Anti-Imperialist

League of 1898 was a mass, populist anti-war organization that opposed the U.S. war with Spain.

The Myth of Right-wing Populism

Until the 1930s, populism was something shunned by those on the far right.

The father of the European far right was Oswald Spengler. His text, "The Decline of the West," was considered the ideological basis of Nazism, Italian fascism, and other mass right-wing movements in 20th century Europe. Spengler's writings describe the need for a tightly organized society in which everyone is assigned a place, authority is sacred, and traditions are unquestioned.

He saw mass popular movements as a sign of societal decay. Julius Evola, the widely influential Italian right-wing ideologue, held similar sentiments. As Marxism and class struggle arose in Europe, those on the far right studied ancient civilizations in India, Tibet, and elsewhere, hoping to discover a "traditionalist" anecdote to rising social chaos.

Hitler, Mussolini, Franco, and other fascist leaders adopted a populist language in the 1930s, seeing it as a way to compete with the mass socialist and communist movements. At this point, one-fifth of the planet was living under a Marxist-Leninist government in the Soviet Union.

Despite populist rhetoric, Hitler's most important ally was the wealthy banker and economist Hjalmar Schacht.

Breaking with the anti-populism and elitism of the right wing, fascists portrayed the political left as a plot by Russia to take over the world. Economic theories like national socialism and corporatism were seen as a way to correct the problems of capitalism, but not surrender to "menace of Bolshevism." "Hitler's Banker," John Weitz's 1997 biography of the Nazi economist and banker Hjalmar Schacht, describes how even as Hitler was emerging in the 1920s, the European right wing was uncomfortable with the populism of the Nazi Party. Weitz quotes German President Paul Hindenburg as commenting "there is too much red on that flag" when seeing the Nazi Party colors.

As the fascists took power, it became pretty clear that the national socialism theory was largely a fiction. In the famous "Night of the Long Knives" Hitler purged the Nazi Party of the more socialistic elements. Figures like Ernst Rohm and Gregor Strasser, who seemed to emphasize the populist rhetoric, were executed.

The economic changes brought about by Hitler's "revolution" involved a lot of military spending, the construction of the autobahn highways, a refusal to pay back foreign debts, and not much else. The industries were not nationalized, though private corporations like Volkswagen certainly benefited from the free labor of prisoners held in concentration camps.

The mass, militant German labor movement was crushed, and workers were forced to join government-controlled unions that were forbidden to strike. The bulk of Germany's wealthy capitalist class — families such as the Krupps, Thyssens, and Schachts — never had their property confiscated. Private bankers continued to enrich themselves. There was really nothing "socialist" about national socialism, aside from some of the pre-1933 rhetoric.

In the United States, the largest mass fascist organization, the Ku Klux Klan, never really raised economic populist demands. Its base was rural whites, and it preached rabid racism, anticommunism, and anti-unionism, and it upheld the sacredness of private property amid its xenophobia.

Among urban anti-communist Catholics in the 1930s, the Silver Legion of America, the Black Legion, the German American Bund, and a variety of bizarre attempts to create a fascist party were carried out. None of these groups were able to gain much traction. Occult novelist William Dudley Pelley's American fascist organization, the Silver Legion of America, focused on anti-Semitism and glorified Mussolini's Italy. Fr. Charles Coughlin's radio broadcasts contained rants about the immorality of capitalism, but always insisted that the answer was a revival of Christianity, not economic reforms.

"Dreamer of the Day," Kevin Coogan's 1999 biography of the fascist ideologue Francis Parker Yockey, emphasizes how uncomfortable many on the far right were with any form of populism. From Oswald Spengler to Julius Evola, the right wing loved authority, order, tradition, obedience, and stability. Class struggle, even waged in the name of nationalism and Christianity, created extreme discomfort among those on the far right.

The major populist voices during the 1930s were not right-wing fascists or nationalists, but socialists and Communists. William Z. Foster campaigned for president in 1932 on a platform of building a

"Soviet America" in which everyone was guaranteed a job, housing, and education. The Communist Party grew to be a major player in American politics during this period. Foster's campaign won over 103,000 votes in the 1932 election, despite being banned from the ballot in many Southern states for advocating racial equality.

Foster was arrested scores of times throughout the campaign, and even describes being tortured for hours by the Los Angeles Police Department in his memoir, "Pages from a Worker's Life." After the campaign he fled to the Soviet Union to recover from extreme physical stress of being arrested nearly 100 times within the span of just a few months.

During this tumultuous decade many well-known figures like Charlie Chaplin, Lillian Hellman, John Steinbeck, Richard Wright, and Paul Robeson

One of the primary populist voices in America during the 1930s was Communist leader William Z. Foster.

joined or worked closely with the massive, left-wing, populist organization known as the Communist Party USA. Starting in 1935, Communists began to emphasize American patriotism, downplaying the idea that they were agents of Moscow, saying "Communism is 20th Century Americanism" and arguing that Presidents Lincoln, Jefferson and Washington might be members of the Communist Party if they were still living.

The Emergence of Left-wing Anti-populism

After World War II, "populism" became kind of a derogatory term in American discourse. Films like "All The King's Men" showed appeals to the common man against the elites as a dangerous demagogic ploy. Books like "Anthem" by Ayn Rand and "1984" by George Orwell glorified the individual, and portrayed communism and fascism as being cut from the same cloth — totalitarian "mass movements" that suppressed individual liberty and freedom.

Alabama Gov. George Wallace, the racist, right-wing, four-time presidential candidate who appealed to Southern whites as working class people and opposed the anti-war and civil rights movements, was deemed a "populist" and denounced by the leaders of both the Republican and Democratic parties.

In the 1970s, the Republican Party adopted some of Wallace's rhetorical style, including his appeal to "common people" against the "cultural elites" who preached anti-racism and social justice. Much has been written about the "Southern Strategy" employed by Republicans, firing up white working class people into a "backlash" against civil rights, and how it contained populistic overtones.

While the right wing toyed with populism during the Cold War, the political left moved away from the messaging style that had defined the Communist Party of the 1930s and the Roosevelt administration. Herbert Marcuse, the well-known Marxist academic of the Frankfurt School, argued that intellectuals, not the working class, were the makers of history.

In May of 1970, New York City witnessed the Hard Hat Riots, in which construction workers attacked anti-war protesters, decrying the left as being middle class and unpatriotic. In this atmosphere, the Weatherman faction of Students for a Democratic Society and other New Left Marxists argued that white Americans were inherently right wing and complicit in the crimes of American imperialism. They sought to organize white, middle-class, counterculture youth to align with the Black Panthers. One of the anthems in the Weatherpeople Songbook, "I'm Dreaming of a White Riot," ends with the couplet: "May you learn to struggle and fight, or the world will off you because you're white."

While the Weathermen approach was less academic, work like J. Sakai's book, "Settlers: The Mythology of the White Proletariat," and Zak Cope's more recent book, "Divided World, Divided Class," put forward the position that white Americans are not workers at all, but exploiters of the third world with no revolutionary potential.

During the Cold War, the U.S. left seemed more to appeal to a kind of alienation among nonconformists than to actual economic suffering.

While certain Marxist-Leninist groups will raise slogans like "Make the Rich Pay" and "A Job Is A Right," to many leftists even today, "anti-capitalism" is a synonym for "anti-consumerism." Radicals and revolutionaries are those who have figuratively "taken the red pill" in the 2000 film "The Matrix." The solution to problems of capitalism is socially conscious shopping and ecology, not organizing the working class against the rich and fighting to seize control the means of production.

The CIA brags on its website about its program known as the "Congress for Cultural Freedom," founded in June of 1950 and dissolved in 1979. The program involved the covert funding of left-wing political activism, music, and art all aimed at redirecting dissidents away from Marxism-Leninism and pro-Soviet politics. The CIA decided it would recruit "a cadre of energetic and well-connected staffers willing to experiment with unorthodox ideas and controversial individuals if that was what it took to challenge the Communists at their own game."

What's Next for American Populism?

Sen. Bernie Sanders' presidential campaign was a rare moment in recent U.S. history. Sanders, who openly called himself a "socialist," was a serious contender for the presidency. He spoke against the "billionaire class" and called for a "political revolution" by the common people, not against gay marriage or flag burning, but against government policies favoring the ultra-rich.

Oddly, articles in U.S. media compared Sanders to Eugene Debs. While both had a left-wing populist appeal, Debs called for an entirely new economic system in which the economy was centrally planned. Sanders called merely for free college and universal health care, paid for with corporate and capital gains taxes.

With Sanders out of the race, and longtime establishment figure Hillary Clinton as the Democratic nominee, many white working class Sanders supporters voted for Trump, especially in Michigan, Wisconsin, Ohio, and Pennsylvania. To many disaffected white workers, populism was all that mattered, whether it had a leftist or right-wing appeal. They were against "the rich" and "the elites." They supported whomever appeared to be most opposed to them.

But will Trump secure populism's place as part of the political right wing? Is left-wing populism dead? Was Sanders' campaign a meaningless outlier?

A lot of this depends on what Trump is able to achieve, not in terms of deportations and police repression, but in terms of reviving the economy. If Trump is able to vastly improve the standard of living among the white working class, especially in the Rust Belt, right-wing nationalist populism will most likely become a longstanding, powerful staple of American politics.

The political left practically invented populism, but since the dawn of the Cold War, socialism, communism, and anti-capitalism have been considered to be largely middle class bohemian trends. However, the changing face of American politics could reverse this. Figures who speak like William Z. Foster, Eugene Debs, or Daniel DeLeon, and rally workers of all different races to fight for their livelihoods and to oppose wars, racism, and empire could re-emerge.

The future character of populism in America is quite unclear, but the next four years are likely to be quite definitive for it.

FASCISM OVER FARMERS?

THE TROUBLING PRIORITIES OF
THE AMERICAN GOVERNMENT

October 10th, 2016 - New Eastern Outlook

US Foods Holding Corporation and Sysco, the two top American food distribution giants, are laying off thousands of workers. Wal-Mart is closing stores and terminating employees. As the price of eggs, beef, cheese, and almost all agricultural products have dropped, farmers across the United States are facing financial ruin.

The ongoing glut in agricultural products is not merely the natural cycle of the market at work. Policies of the US federal government are directly linked to the low food prices. While it is clear that the ongoing agricultural surplus is very bad for the

US public, the government seems to have other priorities.

Broken Promises From Politicians

The agricultural prowess of the United States is known across the planet. The current president of China first visited the United States in 1985. He didn't come to see the Statue of Liberty, or the Washington Monument. Rather, Xi Jinping visited Iowa in order to study the technology and farming techniques employed by some of the most advanced and efficient farmers in the world.

Love for the small farmers is voiced by almost all sectors of US political establishment, and almost always has been. The writings of Thomas Jefferson spoke at length about the "yeoman" and his role in an ideal republic. The left-wing folk singer Pete Seeger sang about how "the farmer is man who feeds them all." Right-wing Radio host Paul Harvey plucked the heart strings of the American public with his "So God Made a Farmer" speech in 1978.

Each election year, American politicians devote special attention to the Iowa caucuses, the first vote in determining who will be the major parties' respective nominees. As they travel across the Midwestern agricultural state, the presidential hopefuls routinely make all kinds of speeches championing "the hard working farmers."

While politicians are known to make promises to the farmers, and seem to recognize that agriculture is essential to the US economy, the policies of recent years, most of them having bipartisan support, have been anything but beneficial to those who work the land. In the current presidential race, Iowa is hotly contested, with Trump and Clinton very close in the polls. The farm glut, spawned by federal policies, is undoubtedly a big factor.

In the first 8 months of 2016, 43 million gallons of milk were poured out due to the glut. According to the Wall Street Journal: "Farmers across the US are pouring out tens of millions of gallons of milk amid massive over glut that has reduced prices and filled warehouses with cheese."

Meanwhile, another WSJ article reports: "Cattle and hog prices hover near the lowest levels in years as U.S. meatpackers produce the largest volume of meat in history."

Between July of 2016 and July of 2017, the price of milk has decreased by 11%. The price of eggs has decreased by 40%.

The overproduction and under-consumption of agricultural products can be directly linked to federal policies. Throughout his administration, Barack Obama has repeatedly cut the Supplemental Nutrition Assistance Program (SNAP) and reduced the amount of food that low income families are able to purchase. The cutting of this federal program directly takes food from the mouths of low-income Americans. Despite the fact that according to the US Department of Agriculture, 13% of American households are now food insecure, the cuts have continued, and hunger is rising among America's poor.

In addition to the obvious impact on low-income Americans, the cuts in food stamps have also cut into food sales. Food producing corporations and small farmers have seen a decrease in their sales. Wal-Mart has laid off thousands of workers and closed thousands of stores. These losses and layoffs can be linked directly to the SNAP cuts.

Congress has recently discussed a plan that would eventually take $150 billion out of the federal food assistance program, a move that would undoubtedly push a lot of food producers, retail employees, and meat packers over the edge, along with many others.

The reductions in food assistance are not the only factor. The economic sanctions against Russia have played a dramatic role in creating the current food glut. The collapse and breaking up of the Soviet Union's collective farm system during the Yeltsin era of the 1990s dramatically reduced Russia's domestic food production. This opened up new markets for American farmers, who greatly increased their exports to the former USSR.

However, the new sanctions imposed in 2014, which restrict US and EU agricultural sales to Russia, have dramatically changed the landscape of the global food market. American farmers have been deprived of 143.5 million potential customers due to the ban on selling to those living in the Russian Federation.

Austerity & Fascism
Leave Farmers Behind

Why is food assistance to low income families being cut? The claim is that the US federal budget is too large, and that hard economic times mandate austerity. However, the United States still has the largest military budget on the planet.

When it comes time to reduce spending, rather than cutting the amount of money spent on tanks, bombs, and drones, the politicians have opted to cut into the nutrition of low-income Americans, along with the livelihoods of farmers and agricultural workers. The thousands of military bases around the world, along with the billions given in foreign military aid to countries like Israel, all seem be far more important to US leaders.

And why has the US drastically restricted the exporting agricultural products to Russia? The sanctions were enacted in 2014, in response to the Ukraine crisis. The elected President of Ukraine, Victor Yanukovich, was toppled in orgy of street violence. The new government, with a base of support only in the western regions of the country, has within its ranks many open admirers of Adolf Hitler, and is very hostile to Russia.

Since 2014, the people of Eastern Ukraine have taken up arms to resist the new regime. The people in the region of Crimea voted to become apart of the Russian Federation, whose military they had been hosting since the collapse of the USSR. Sanctions were imposed on Russia and continue, based on allegations that Russia is supporting the resistance of people in the Eastern regions against the new, pro-Western regime. US leaders tell us the sanctions are intended to punish Russia for "meddling" in Ukraine.

Since the passing of the sanctions, Russia has revived its own domestic agricultural programs. Small farmers across Russia are producing beef, wheat, and other products no longer sold to them by the US and the EU. Russian agriculture has experienced a boom since 2014, and Russian President Vladimir Putin is even more popular than prior to the crisis.

The decision of US leaders to wage economic warfare against Russia in support of Ukrainian fascists, while at the same time cutting assistance to low-income American families, is contrary to values often displayed throughout American history. Both Lincoln and Roosevelt saw prosperity for the agricultural heartland of the United States and the millions who lived in it as vitally important for the entire country. These two most beloved Presidents in US history both worked closely in alliance with small farmers, often in opposition to Wall Street bankers with different interests.

The rallying cry of the Republican Party in its early years, was "Free Land, Free Labor, Free Men!" The "Free Soilers," farmers who wanted to halt the expansion of slavery in new US territories were an essential part of it. While slavery found support in the financial districts of London and New York, the small farmers had a material interest in ending the barbaric practice, and anti-slavery militias appeared in Iowa and Kansas years before the Civil War broke out.

It was a broad coalition of small farmers, religious abolitionists, and organized labor that eventually put Abraham Lincoln into the White House where he was forced to battle the slaveholders. The process that unfolded recreated the country, in what is widely called "The Second American Revolution."

"An American Government Cannot Allow Americans To Starve"

The programs that preceded the currently existing Supplemental Nutritional Assistance Program (SNAP) were the brainchild of Secretary of Agriculture Henry Wallace, who eventually became the Vice President. When the first "food stamps" were issued in 1939, the director of the program, Milo Perkins described it this way: "We got a picture of a gorge, with farm surpluses on one cliff and under-nourished city folks with outstretched hands on the other. We set out to find a practical way to build a bridge across that chasm."

While Roosevelt was universally hated by Wall Street bankers, he was very popular with organized labor, artists and musicians, as well as small farmers. As the unemployment councils and labor unions fought for a better life across the country, Roosevelt aligned himself with the mass movement in the streets. Essential in Roosevelt's progressive coalition was the US Communist

Party, an organization that sought to build a "Workers and Farmer's Government." When big business objected to Roosevelt's dramatic economic reforms, he defended them by saying "An American government cannot allow Americans to Starve."

Roosevelt later aligned with the Russian people in order to defeat Adolf Hitler. FDR's opposition to fascism and his policies of feeding of hungry Americans while subsidizing farmers were not isolated from each other.

They corresponded with his overall view of the world, expressed in 1944: "We cannot be content, no matter how high that general standard of living may be, if some fraction of our people—whether it be one-third or one-fifth or one-tenth- is ill-fed, ill-clothed, ill housed, and insecure….We have come to a clear realization of the fact that true individual freedom cannot exist without economic security and independence….People who are hungry and out of a job are the stuff of which dictatorships are made."

In 2016, things are very different. While banks were bailed out without hesitation during the 2008 financial crisis, financial assistance to low income Americans continues to be cut. Wall Street and London see the Eurasian Bloc of Russia and China as a rising competitor to their financial hegemony. The wealthy financial elite largely support sanctions and further isolation of both countries despite whatever disastrous impact on American farmers, agricultural workers, and food distributors.

Children across the United States are hungry, as 13% of households are food insecure, according to the US Department of Agriculture. Farm workers and those who work for food distributors and supermarkets are losing their jobs. Gallons of milk are at this moment being dumped out in hopes of raising the prices, while food warehouses sit filled with rotting, unsold cheese.

Meanwhile, US and NATO forces are increasing their presence in Eastern Europe, threatening Russia. As agricultural sanctions on Russia continue, weapons and training are being provided to a Ukrainian military that is known to contain a number fascist sympathizers, including the infamous Avoz Battalion.

As discontent rises in the United States, it is largely centered in the agricultural and de-industrialized mid-western heartland. It is clear that many Americans desperately want something to change. A government that prioritizes fascism in Ukraine over farmers in Iowa, Wisconsin, and Ohio, is clearly out of touch.

Part Three:
The Aftermath

THE LAST DAYS OF OBAMA:

NAPOLEONIC MANEUVERS AT THE SECURITY COUNCIL

January 23rd, 2017 - New Eastern Outlook

It seemed to come almost out of nowhere. The United States usually protects Israel from critical resolutions at the UN Security Council. However, in a dramatic move, the US abstained and a resolution criticizing recent settlement activity was passed by the 15-member body.

But this was not the end. John Kerry, Obama's former Secretary of State, gave a lengthy address a few days later. Kerry's speech was not so different from the statements of previous leaders, both Democrats and Republicans. He defended Israel's existence, and denounced almost all forces actively opposing Israel.

However, Kerry harshly criticized specific Israeli policies. While Kerry's speech defending the UN abstention uttered the standard, mildly critical, pro-Israeli talking points, it did contain some words that, taken out of context and spread throughout the internet, could and did indeed make a lot of Israelis and Zionists very angry. The most quoted one was: ""If the choice is one state, Israel can either be Jewish or democratic, it cannot be both."

Kerry was alluding to the fact that if Palestinians are absorbed into Israel in a "one state solution" but Israel remains a "Jewish State" this will not be democratic. According to Kerry, under such circumstances Palestinians would be second class citizens, i.e. non-Jews in a Jewish state. Immediately, Kerry's speech was decried by Israelis. Netanyahu fired back, as did the entire pro-Israeli blogosphere. The Republican and Likud Party aligned voices escalated the shrill accusations that Obama was a secret Muslim, a member of the Muslim brotherhood, a terrorist sympathizer, a Neo-Nazi, a Communist, and everything else he has been called for 8 years straight.

Meanwhile, Israel did not stop its settlement activity, and was not really affected at all by the

The Obama administration maintained US support for both the Saudi monarchy and Israel.

resolution. The billions of dollars in US aid to Israel continued. Obama has left the office on January 20th, and is now replaced by Donald Trump, who claims to be more pro-Israel than Obama. The UN Security Council is not taking any specific action to halt the settlement activities condemned in its resolution.

Nothing really changed, but a lot of dramatic, heated words were exchanged between the USA and its closest Middle Eastern ally. Why did this happen?

Napoleon & Obama:
"I Come to Restore Your Rights"

In 1798, the French militarist Napoleon
Bonaparte, who seized power in the aftermath of
the revolution and eventually became Emperor,
set out to conquer Egypt. He issued a
proclamation saying:

"People of Egypt! You will be told by our enemies
that I am come to destroy your religion. Believe
them not. Tell them I am come to restore your
rights, punish your usurpers, and revive the true
worship of Mohammed. Tell them that I venerate,
more than do the Mamelukes, God, his prophet,
and the Koran."

Among the people of Egypt and Syria, as well as
the entire Arab world, there was deep hatred for
the British and Ottoman empires, who functioned
as Napoleon's rivals. Napoleon hoped that he
could convince Muslims throughout the region to
support him, and on this basis that he could defeat
their hated colonial enemies, and conquer the
region for France.

Napoleon was lying. He was not an adherent of
the Islamic faith. Some speculate that he may have
been a freemason, and became familiar with the
Koran and Islam due to their inclusion in Masonic

rituals. Regardless, years later, Napoleon explained the proclamation to his fellow French Christians saying:

"A change of religion, inexcusable for the sake of private interests, becomes comprehensible when immense political results are involved.... Do you think the Empire of the East and perhaps the subjugation of the whole of Asia was not worth a turban and some loose trouser? The state of feeling in the army was such that it would have undoubtedly lent itself to a joke."

Barack Obama, like Napoleon Bonaparte, is not a Muslim. As offensive and heretical as some evangelical Christians and Catholics may consider the teachings of the United Church of Christ and Reverend Jeremiah Wright, they are not Islamic in any conceivable way. Barack Obama was married in a church. He has been photographed drinking wine and eating hot dogs.

Obama's middle name is "Hussein." As a child, while living in Indonesia, he attended an Islamic elementary school. Obama apparently did meet with the Palestinian-American professor Edward Said. With all of this to cite as evidence, the allegation that he was a "secret Muslim" has not vanished.

The endless, semi-hysterical attacks on Obama for having alleged links to Islam certainly had an impact outside of US borders. This impact may not have been accidental. Writing in the Atlantic Monthly in 2007, the self-described conservative Andrew Sullivan considered the colorful background of the future president to be an asset:

"What does he offer? First and foremost: his face. Think of it as the most effective potential re-branding of the United States since Reagan. Such a re-branding is not trivial—it's central to an effective war strategy… The next president has to create a sophisticated and supple blend of soft and hard power to isolate the enemy, to fight where necessary, but also to create an ideological template that works to the West's advantage over the long haul. There is simply no other candidate with the potential of Obama to do this."

Sullivan's widely read and cited article said: "If you wanted the crudest but most effective weapon against the demonization of America that fuels Islamist ideology, Obama's face gets close. It proves them wrong about what America is in ways no words can."

The USA certainly had a lot of credibility to regain as the Bush era came to an end. The unilateral invasion of Iraq had been widely opposed, not just in the Middle East, but even among NATO states. Bush had gone as far as to say "this crusade, this war on terrorism, is going to take a while." The word "crusade" doesn't exactly bring up pleasant feelings among Muslims around the world.

Meanwhile, the federal agencies of the United States flew into a very Islamophobic mode after the 9/11 attacks. The leaders of a religious charity known as the "Holy Land Foundation" were imprisoned for nothing other than running soup kitchens for Palestinian children. Mosques across the United States were then and continue to be widely surveilled.

His Middle Name is "Hussein"

Voices like Andrew Sullivan's hoped that Obama's background could restore the credibility of the USA in the eyes of Muslims. But this was just the tip of the iceberg. What came about in the first term of the Obama administration? In 2011 the world watched the "Arab Spring." Across the Middle East, impoverished people rose up against their governments.

Analysts often argue that the Arab Spring was spawned by the global financial crisis and the regional drought. Throughout the Arab world, crops failed, water was scarce, and impoverished people piled into the cities facing dire economic conditions. The uprisings that eventually erupted were predictable. Such conditions are known to spark unrest.

But the world did not see a repeat of the 1979 Iranian Revolution, where the Persians toppled a western puppet dictator under the slogans of "Not Capitalism but Islam" and "War of Poverty Against Wealth." The western capitalist apparatus was ready. The Arab Spring was immediately redirected to serve their ends. Social media outlets based in western countries, and the global apparatus of pro-American NGOs swung into action.

With a commander-in-chief who most people in the Middle East had a favorable opinion of, the forces of global power were able to ensure that the revolt did not become an uprising against western capitalism. No new anti-imperialist regimes were born. Rather, the opposite happened.

In Egypt, the pro-US regime of Hosni Mubarak fell, but what replaced it? First, Egypt elected Mohamed Morsi, a leader of the CIA-linked Muslim Brotherhood. Morsi was then toppled by a military coup d'etat. Now General Sisi, a top military leader under Mubarak, is in power.

The US backed Saudi regime was allowed to crush the uprisings within its own borders. Ayatollah Nimr Al-Nimr, a Shia cleric who led protests demanding civil liberties and religious freedom in the country was eventually beheaded for his role in the Arab spring. Saudi troops poured into Bahrain to keep the monarchy in power and crush the Shia majority that demanded their rights. In the aftermath of the revolt, Yemen staged a sham election in which Mansour Hadi, a Saudi puppet, was the only candidate on the ballot. Yemen is now torn apart by war, as many Yemenis reject Hadi's pro-Saudi and Pro-US regime.

The energy and momentum of the Arab Spring, amplified and directed by the western TV networks along with Twitter and Facebook, went toward targeting two anti-imperialist, socialist governments. Gaddafi's Libya had the highest life expectancy in Africa. Syria's Bashar Assad presides over a centrally planned economy, supports Palestinian resistance, and is aligned with Iran, Russia and China.

In both Libya and Syria the United States began actively working to transform the Arab Spring into a successful regime change operation. Though the faces promoted on western television were often middle class, secular young people who dreamed of American consumerism while mouthing words about "democracy," the brute force behind the Syrian and Libyan "revolutions" were religious extremists.

Based from the Syrian and Libyan countryside, forces linked to Al-Queda and the Muslim Brotherhood were joined by many foreign Jihadist fighters from throughout the region. The forces who toppled the Libyan government and continue to fight against the Syrian Arab Republic are dominated by those who adhere to Wahabbism, the ideology of Saudi Arabia and Osama Bin Laden. These deeply religious forces, working to topple anti-imperialist governments, happily took guns and funding from a country led by a man who went to a Muslim school, met with Edward Said, and whose middle name happened to be "Hussein."

Imagine what could have happened in the region, if the wave of uprisings had taken place while George Bush "the crusader" was still in office. Obama's presidency played a decisive role in manipulating and redirecting the events of 2011.

Netanyahu vs. Obama: A Made For TV Drama

It is not uncommon for celebrities to clash with each other in the public arena. Often, these fights are not spontaneous, but intentionally provoked, or even planned, in order to generate publicity for both parties involved. For example, long before running for President, Donald Trump captured the attention of news headlines by having a spat with TV personality Rosie O'Donnell.

The perceived tension between Benjamin Netanyahu and Barack Obama has the looks of a "made for TV drama." It is a prolonged public spat that is mutually beneficial to both parties. Do they actually dislike each other when the cameras are not rolling? Who knows.

While Obama and Netanyahu have butted heads, the US aid to Israel has not decreased or been cut off. Under Obama, the United States has worked to topple the Baathist Syrian government, one of Israel's primary regional opponents. Israel has supported the regime change efforts with airstrikes in Syria targeting anti-ISIS fighters in the Hezbollah organization.

Obama's supposed feud with Israeli Prime Minister Benjamin Netanyahu was mutually beneficial in terms of public relations. Israel never stopped receiving US funding or support during Obama's presidency.

The 2011 NATO intervention in Libya, championed loudly from the White House, toppled the Islamic Socialist government that had a long record of opposing Israel and arming Palestinian resistance.

Obama boasts that he has ended Iran's peaceful nuclear energy program, and is making Israel safer from a supposed Iranian threat in the process. While there is occasionally criticism of Israel's settlement activities, they continue unabated. However, Obama's clash with Netanyahu plays well for him, and the United States, in the Arab world. Throughout the Middle East, Netanyahu and Tel-Aviv are the most hated villains. Obama's trading of nasty words with Israeli leaders raises the credibility of the United States. It gives the United States a kind of distance from Israel on the international stage, while US support remains key and keeps flowing in without pause. Obama's Department of Justice has even conducted raids against pro-Palestinian activists.

Netanyahu benefits from the spat as well. Fear and hatred of Palestinians, Muslims, and Arabs has been key in securing the recent electoral victories of the Likud Party. If Netanyahu looked like he was friendly toward someone who attended an Islamic elementary school, or had the middle name "Hussein" this would discredit him in the eyes of his base.

Despite the fact that Israel receives billions of dollars from the United States, as well as weapons and other assistance, Netanyahu looks as if he is not afraid to bite the hand that feeds him. Fighting with Obama allows Netanyahu to look like a brave, fearless, true believer in the Zionist cause.

"Don't Forget About Obama!"

Though many Israelis and supporters of Israel in the United States dislike Donald Trump, he has presented himself during the campaign as a pro-Israeli hardliner. His speech to the American Israeli Public Affairs Committee was a repetition of standard pro-Israeli talking points, saying: "When you live in a society where the firefighters are the heroes, little kids want to be firefighters… In Palestinian society, the heroes are those who murder Jews."

Trumps statements about banning Muslim immigration haven't exactly been popular in the Arab world. Statements like "Islam hates us" don't go over so well either.

The fear among certain forces in the United States is that Trump could alienate the many Muslim allies of the United States in the Arab world. Wall Street oil companies make lots of money from the various autocratic regimes in Qatar, Kuwait, Saudi Arab, UAE, and elsewhere. Pentagon weapons manufacturers also make lots of money from selling their hardware to these regimes.

Like Napoleon's strategy in Egypt, efforts to portray Obama as sympathizer with Muslims and Arabs haven't exactly worked out so well. While the elites within the US aligned Gulf States and some of extremists forces who have poured into Syria have bought into the idea Obama is a trustworthy ally, many people in the region have not. The Syrian government has not fallen. Iran has not really been weakened.

The economic problems and other factors that fueled the discontent of 2011 have not vanished. There is no guarantee that the oil bankers of the United States will keep their grip over this vastly important territory. Certain sectors harbor real fear that Trump's brash tone could now ruin everything.

The last minute moves at the UN Security Council, publicly invoking Israel's wrath, was a message to the Arab world. It was a desperate, final attempt to say: "Whatever Trump does, don't forget about Obama! Not all Americans are hardline supporters of Israel! Not everyone in Washington hates the Arabs! Muslims of the world, keep trusting us, don't turn against America!"

AN OPEN LETTER TO THE J20 PROTESTERS

January 20th, 2017 - Mint Press News

These are not emotionless times in the United States of America. Anger is running high all across the country. If you have a moment, I urge you to calmly please consider just a few things I have to say. I'm not a Trump supporter, but I have some deep reservations about the "Anti-Trump" movement.

First, you are absolutely right to be offended, angry, and triggered by Donald Trump's words, and his victory in November. The statements he has made about about immigrants, Muslims, and women are unacceptable. His calls for massive deportations and his support for the police despite their record of brutality is not something any progressive can support.

Secondly, freedom of speech is essential. Any repression or brutality reigned down on protesters must be loudly opposed. Americans have the right to protest against the commander in chief, and this should never be compromised.

But while you are protesting, please consider the following points:

1. Millions of Americans voted for Donald Trump. Are many of them racist, sexist, homophobic, transphobic, xenophobic, or otherwise bigoted? Perhaps. But shouldn't you be trying to win these people away from these views that you consider to be problematic? Do you think you are going to win them over by just shouting "racist!" and "bigot" at them? Not everyone has the same opportunities. Not all Americans get to attend expensive universities, take courses in race and gender studies, learn to confront their inner prejudices, and become educated progressives. A lot of working class people in Ohio, Pennsylvania, Wisconsin, and Michigan, frankly don't know what you mean when you call them racist or transphobic. Shouldn't you be trying to change their views with clear, precise arguments, not hateful, condescending vitriol?

2. Do really you think bigotry is the only thing that caused millions of Americans to vote for Trump? His campaign also involved talk of bringing back good paying industrial jobs to the rustbelt. He spoke about ending regime change operations around the world and working toward global peace. He spoke about rebuilding the infrastructure of the country. Who knows if Trump really means any of this, and for everything he has said, there are words and actions to the contrary. But aren't these things that you, as a progressive, also believe in?

If millions of Americans are angry about a lack of jobs, endless wars, and crumbling infrastructure, why is it that Donald Trump is the one capturing their anger? Trump even spoke about "international bankers."

Why is it that amid rising anti-capitalist sentiments, the right-wing, not leftists like yourself, is leading the populist charge? Isn't this your territory? Shouldn't people who are angry at Wall Street become socialists, anarchists, or communists? Is it possible that perhaps Trump's rise shows that maybe you are doing something wrong?

3. The Democrats big argument against Trump is that he is somehow connected to Russia. Obama imposed new sanctions on Russia, in response to alleged meddling in the elections, which many Democrats blame for Trump's victory. Signs at previous anti-Trump rallies have said "No Putin President" and "Trump Works for the Kremlin." As a leftist, you should know what Mccarthyism is. Why is it that the Anti-Trump movement, which you now support, is preaching Mccarthyism? Are you comfortable with that?

I hope you will take the time to consider these three points. If your goal tomorrow is to feel good about yourself, get your voice heard, and then return to business as usual, I suspect you will achieve it.

But if you actually want to make things better in America, and end the rising chaos, poverty, and the emerging low wage police state, I urge you think a little deeper. Instead of thinking about just how you can make yourself feel superior to those who support Trump, perhaps you should reconsider the tactics and rhetoric the organized left has used in the last 30 years.

The country is far bigger than the East Coast and Southern California. Millions of Americans are angry and desperately want change. Millions of them voted for Trump because they were led to believe he would bring that change.

Its quite trendy and easy to be anti-Trump in certain parts of the country. The economy in New York City and southern California is much better than elsewhere. But across the USA, a lot of people are hurting. Heroin addiction, suicide, and other diseases of despair are killing people off.

The rise of figures like Alex Jones shows that more and more people are looking for answers beyond mainstream political discourse.
Isn't it worth at least having a conversation with these people? Should all the rising anger among low income white people, much of it about the very issues your ideologies claim to be addressing, be simply handed over to the right-wing?

Are you satisfied with the left remaining an isolated book club of middle class bohemians? Or do you actually want a new America?

Best,

Caleb T. Maupin

EXECUTIVE ORDERS & AIRPORT PROTESTS

February 6th, 2017 - New Eastern Outlook

Trump signed an executive order. Airports filled up with protesters. The media screamed about a Muslim ban. Federal Judges intervened. Anger and chaos erupted.

What is actually going on? The answers from both sides of the political spectrum are loaded with emotion and lacking truthful content.

"Trump is trying to protect us from terrorists! He's keeping the Muslims out of our country!" shout Trump's defenders. Well, no terrorist attack on US soil has ever been carried out by anyone from the 7 countries restricted. The countries that have been linked to recent terrorist attacks, such as Saudi Arabia and Afghanistan, are not included.

"Trump is a racist! He's banning Muslims! We can't block people because of their religion!" Scream the liberal protesters. Well, many Muslim majority countries such as Turkey and Indonesia are not included in the ban. Furthermore, the ban applies to all people from these countries, not just Muslims. The Syrian Arab Republic, for example, is home to many Christians, Druze, and even a small Jewish community. The Islamic Republic of Iran has a large population of Armenian Christians, Jews, and many adherents to an ancient faith called Zoroastrianism. All of these non-Muslims are also subject to the ban.

One contributing factor to the outburst of rage is the crass, sudden, "slap in the face" nature of the executive order. Until the administration backed down, even green-card holding permanent residents were being turned away at airports, something that definitely caused anguish and panic among many people.

Calling It A "Muslim Ban" – Good for Trump & the Democrats

Throughout his Presidential election campaign, Trump repeatedly appealed to contempt and distrust of those who practice Islam. He talked about "banning Muslims" from entering the USA. His speech to the American Israeli Public Affairs Committee included a lot of pandering to Anti-

Islamic sentiments. Millions of working class people in rural and suburban areas voted for Trump, because of these very statements. In the aftermath of 9/11 many Americans have come to see all adherents of the Islamic faith as a single scary, foreign, violent group.

The idea that Trump would enact a "Muslim ban" is something that will increase, not decrease his credibility to millions of the middle aged right-wing working class whites who voted for him in rustbelt and southern states. It plays into Trump's well crafted image as a bold defender of the common man, who is not politically correct, and unafraid of being scorned by elitist urban liberals. However, as much as it would please his right-wing, anti-Islamic base, and as much as his opponents proclaim it in condemnation, the reality is that Trump has not enacted a Muslim ban.

Donald Trump has temporarily suspended entrance to the United States from seven countries: Yemen, Syria, Iraq, Iran, Somalia, Libya, and Sudan. Now the US public is having a heated argument about a "Muslim Ban." Opponents call it bigoted, supporters call it bold, and neither side acknowledges reality.

Observers of American politics should be reminded of the healthcare debate in the early years of the Obama administration. The Affordable Care Act or "Obamacare" was not universal healthcare or socialized medicine, and did very little to change the country's private healthcare system. However, the right-wing rallied against it, proclaiming it was socialism, and the left rallied in its defense, employing socialistic rhetoric. Both sides of the American political spectrum clashed with each other, accepting a similar fictional narrative about the Affordable Care Act.

The Non-Spontaneous Airport Protests

After this sudden action, much like the healthcare debate, "the gloves have come off." In 2009, Tea Partiers responded to the Affordable Care Act by displaying firearms at townhall meetings and engaging in other acts of protest that are normally considered "out of bounds." In response to Trump, the Democratic Party apparatus mobilized its supporters to protest inside of airports. The demonstrations were mobilized very rapidly, and got intense with people being arrested, and maced with pepper spray at various locations.

Those who pretend that the protests were completely random, unplanned, or spontaneous are completely delusional. Airports are among the most free speech restricted locations in the country. While decades ago it was permitted to pass out political leaflets or petition at airports, courts long ago forbid such things. Under normal circumstances it is illegal, not only to engage in protest or "public disturbance" at an airport, but even to video record inside one.

Yet, without any widespread public announcement or organizing, thousands of Democratic Party activists flooded into airports for some rather rowdy protests. Under normal circumstances doing such things would result in immediate arrest and perhaps even terrorism charges. Not only did the police not arrest the initial protesters, but they allowed the demonstrations to grow bigger and bigger. Though videotaping is not permitted in airports, live streaming videos found their way on to social media, and TV news cameras conveniently found their way in as well.

In many countries when the elected government is toppled by the military, one of the first actions taken is seizing the airports. One could even read into the sudden mobilizations, clearly supported by some of the most powerful people in Democratic Party, a veiled threat of a military coup d'etat.

The CIA Strikes Back

But why was there such a swift response to Trump's action? Why did the Democratic Party unleash its forces so rapidly in response to Trump's move? Are the Democrats like Hillary Clinton, who tweeted in support of the protests, simply humanitarians who hold deep compassion for immigrants?

The real answer can be found, subtly, in the news coverage surrounding the opposition to the ban. This mainstream news reports shows an Iraqi family blocked by Trump's move, and describes how the father had "risked his life to support the United States" and his family was rewarded with a visa. This is not an uncommon practice. Allies of the United States in conflicts around the world are routinely rewarded with visas. The US military has many "green card soldiers" from Latin America, who are attempting to gain legal residency in the USA by serving in the military.

In each of the 7 countries listed in the ban, there are thousands of individuals who have collaborated with the United States in order to carry out foreign policy goals. In Syria, for example, hundreds of thousands of Wahabbi extremists have been working to topple the government. In Iraq, Saudi Arabia has cooperated with the United States in efforts to roll back Iranian influence among the Shia communities. In Yemen, Al-Queda, Saudi Arabia, and the United States are all working to topple the Revolutionary Committees aligned with the Ansarullah organization, commonly called the "Houthis."

The individuals who have collaborated with the United States in the 7 countries are often Muslims, who adhere to an interpretation of the faith similar to that of Saudi Arabia or of the Muslim Brotherhood.

In the aftermath of the executive order, it has been revealed that Trump is openly discussing a formal ban of the Muslim Brotherhood, and designating it as a terrorist organization.While many countries, including Russia and Saudi Arabia, already outlaw the Brotherhood, the USA does not.

In fact, the Muslim Brotherhood has been a key ally of the United States in the Middle East for decades. The Brotherhood worked with the CIA to destabilize Abdul Nasser's anti-imperialist, socialist government in Egypt. The Brotherhood staged a violent uprising against the Syrian Arab Republic during the 1980s, and has been aligned with anti-government militants in the current Syrian civil war. The Muslim Brotherhood enthusiastically worked with the Obama administration to topple Moammar Gaddafi and reduce Libya to chaos and poverty.

The Muslim Brotherhood functions across the Middle East. The reigning monarchy of Qatar, which also sponsors the TV network known as Al-Jazeera, is a key financial backer of the Muslim Brotherhood. The CIA has worked for decades to maintain the US government's relationship with the Muslim Brotherhood, seeing them as allies or proxies in the fight against anti-imperialist, nationalist, and socialist governments in the region.

While the CIA sees the Muslim Brotherhood as a useful ally, other key players in US society disagree. The Israeli government and its network of supporters have deep contempt for the Muslim Brotherhood, due to the fact that its Palestinian affiliate, Hamas, is their battlefield enemy. Other figures in the security apparatus and the military see the Brotherhood as a threat due to its record of assassinations and terrorism.

Trump's recent move indicates that he may represent a section of the US elite that wants to terminate the relationship between the US government and the Muslim Brotherhood, as well as various Wahabbi fanatics. The CIA, on the other hand, feels that is very important to maintain these alliances which it has worked on for many decades. This disagreement among the most powerful leaders in the United States is the basis on which the sudden executive order, and the sweeping protests at the airports, has taken place.

Soros, Brzezinski & Brennan

John Brennan was Obama's CIA director. He oversaw drone strikes that killed civilians. He worked toward the goal of overthrowing independent nationalist governments in places like Libya and Syria, among others. Brennan has done all of this, and can be called many things by those who disagree with such policies. One thing that he cannot accurately be called is "conservative."

John Brennan admits that in 1976 he voted for Gus Hall, the Presidential candidate of the Communist Party USA. Starting in 1996 he directed the CIA station in Saudi Arabia's capital city, Riyahl. Unproven statements from ex-FBI agent and others claim that he even converted to Wahabbi Islam while working from this post.

The CIA's strategy for achieving US foreign policy goals and those who carry them out often appear to be very liberal and unorthodox. Many naively assume that those who work for American intelligence and security agencies are hardline conservatives due to the nature of the job, but in reality, many individuals linked to CIA are associated with left-wing causes.

In the rhetoric of Trump supporters and the right-wing, the name "George Soros" shows up frequently. Those who defend the airport protests have mocked this rhetoric, saying things such as "He owes me money, I haven't been paid" etc. Though liberals often want to reduce him to a gag-line, George Soros is a very real person, not a fixture of the right-wing's imagination. The far left, especially socialists and communists, should know him very well.

Soros is one of the CIA's most important allies. He is a billionaire who helped to topple the various Marxist-Leninist governments across

Eastern Europe. Soros funneled money to the Polish anti-Communist "Solidarity" trade union movement. He also funded the anti-Communist "Charter 77" movement in Czechoslovakia, as well as dissidents who worked toward bringing about the collapse of the Soviet Union in 1991.

Soros, like those who run the National Endowment for Democracy, the Tides Foundation, the Open Society Institute and other liberal foundations, appears to have coordinated his funding of activism around the world with the strategies of the Central Intelligence Agency. When the CIA was working against the Serbian government, Soros funded the Kosovo Independence Movement. When US foreign policy strategists targeted Alexander Lukashenko, calling Belarus 'the last Soviet Republic,' Soros money went to "activists" in that country.

CIA operative and Presidential Medal of Freedom winner Zbigniew Brzezinski, like Soros and Brennan, cannot be described as "conservative" or "right-wing." Brzezinski bragged that he gave the Soviet Union "its Vietnam" by luring them into Afghanistan. Today, his daughter Mika Brzezinski is a host on the liberal, Democratic Party aligned cable TV network MSNBC.

George Soros and Zbigniew Brzezinski are identified with specific foreign policy strategies developed during the Cold War. The strategy is that rather than directly attacking countries with the military, governments and leaders that are disliked by Wall Street can be toppled through the funding of dissident movements, information warfare, economic sanctions, the facilitation of chaos, and "color revolutions."

Deceptions About Iran

Trump's swift moves and those within the state apparatus who oppose it hold strategic disagreements with each other related to world events. One obvious disagreement between Trump and his predecessor relates to the Islamic Republic of Iran.

Thousands of Christians openly practice their faith inside the Islamic Republic of Iran.

Trump's executive order was followed up by an announcement that Iran is "on notice." New sanctions were placed on Iran. Many times throughout his campaign, Trump spoke against Iran with very heated words.

Many of Trump's supporters believe that somehow the Islamic Republic of Iran, Al-Queda, and ISIL are cut from the same cloth or somehow linked to each other.

The reality is that the Islamic Republic of Iran is one of ISIL's biggest enemies. ISIL, Al-Queda, and other Wahabbi extremists call the Iranians "Shia Apostates." They seek to violently overthrow the Islamic Republic and slaughter those who live within its borders. Iranian Revolutionary Guards are on the battlefield in Syria each day, alongside Syrian government forces who are fighting against ISIL.

Iran is one of the most stable countries within the region. Inside Iran's borders, Sunnis, Christian, Zoroastrians, and Jews are free to practice their faith under the Shia-led government. Consistent with its founder Imam Khomeni's calls for "Not Capitalism, But Islam" the Islamic Republic has an economy that is tightly controlled by the state and ensures housing, education, and healthcare for the population. Iran's state owned oil corporations competes with Wall Street on the global markets, and uses the proceeds to develop its independent economy. Iran supports the Syrian government in an effort to end the wave of Wahabbi terrorism that has flowed into the country.

Obama and the CIA seem to have believed that the best approach toward Iran involved negotiations, support for internal dissidents, and friendly diplomatic gestures. The Trump administration, by including Iran in its recent ban, and repeating anti-Iranian rhetoric, seems to believe in a more directly confrontational approach.

When it comes to US foreign policy, the recent executive order and the dramatic response to it, lay bare the fact that there is great disagreement within the halls of power. As the delusion of a unipolar world is being so obviously eroded, independent countries with planned economies emerge, and the world continues to see an economic crisis, such intense disagreements among the ruling elite of the United States are to be expected.

REVIEWING 2016:
AMERICAN INDIVIDUALISM IN
CRISIS

January 3rd, 2017 - SP News

When looking over the newsworthy events that took place in the United States throughout 2016, a common thread ties many of them together. So many major events illustrate a real failure of the powers that be to solve problems.

And these problems are not new. The epidemic of opiate addiction has been brewing since the 1990s when American doctors, incentivized by medical drug manufacturers, began over-prescribing pain killers. The crisis intensified when the US invasion of Afghanistan unleashed the country's poppy growers, flooding the market, and driving the price down.

Now, cheap heroin is everywhere and people are dying. In 2015, more Americans died from drug overdose than from gun violence, another problem plaguing America. As 2016 comes to a close, the numbers of drug-related deaths are still rising.

The Pulse nightclub shooting broke records in 2016 for America's ongoing problem of gun violence. Mass shootings, in which deranged individuals with guns begin slaughtering people, have become a regular occurrence in recent years. Many times President Barack Obama has appeared on television to comfort a grieving nation and call for tighter gun control. The present order is unable to adequately address the issue, and the shootings continue.

Guns, Racism & Discontent

One could say that problems related to race are almost a built-in problem for the United States, which defined African enslaved persons as 3/5 of a human being in its Constitution. Since the end of slavery, after a bloody civil war, there have been endless protests, tensions, and controversies, both violent and peaceful, related to racial questions.

The death of Muhammad Ali, the world heavyweight boxing champion who had aligned himself with Black nationalism and converted to Islam during the 1960s, gave the country a moment to reflect on the long history of racial strife.

2016 is the final year of the presidency of Barack Obama. His presidency began with so much optimism about a "post racial society" and the belief that this age-old source of disagreement on the American continent could be finally resolved with a dark skinned man as commander in chief. This final year of Obama's presidency is notable for illustrating how one blatantly unfulfilled these expectations.

Protests swept Charlotte, North Carolina in response to the killing of Keith Lamont Scott by police. The country nervously watched as unrest swept yet another city, with fresh memories of the violence that swept Baltimore and Ferguson in the previous year.

In addition to the thousands of peaceful protests, in Baton Rouge, Louisiana, and Dallas, Texas, police officers were shot and killed by individuals who were angry about the documented wave of unpunished police brutality. After these shootings, many mostly white Americans, who had been almost silent during the continuous wave of "Black Lives Matter" protests, expressed sympathy for police. A huge gap in public opinion became very apparent.

The isolated, violent individuals who were outraged by police brutality were certainly not the only Americans to express their political views with firearms. The year of 2016 began with the seizure of federal property from January 2nd to February 11th by "sovereign citizens" and right-wing militia organizations in Oregon. A shootout with the FBI and state police eventually ensued. One of the armed militants was killed, and 27 were arrested. Gun-toting, right-wing organizations that talk of "constitutional liberties" and opposing the federal government are notably present across the US.

A Twist in American Politics

The 2016 presidential election, much like the increase of protests and political gun battles, revealed how divided, and desperate the country is. Bernie Sanders, a US senator from Vermont who describes himself as a "socialist," long a forbidden term in Americana, was welcomed onto the national political stage.

Millions of Americans voted for Sanders in the Democratic presidential primary. Leaked emails showed that the Democratic National Committee was working behind the scenes to ensure his defeat, and secure the nomination for longtime party power broker Hillary Clinton. The revelations showed a kind of cynical and dishonest internal atmosphere at the top of the Democratic Party, and therefore disillusioned many activists. Sanders' challenge within the Democratic Party seemed mild compared to Trump's complete shake-up of the Republican Party. Donald Trump, a New York City real estate tycoon and billionaire, who declared his candidacy was at first treated almost as a joke, but ultimately won the election.

Trump's campaign used crass language, demonized Muslims and immigrant workers, opposed international trade deals, and criticized the failures of US military interventions. With slogans like, "America First" and "Make America Great Again," Trump won the electoral college vote, despite proof of a solid majority of voters favoring Clinton.

Neither Trump nor Sanders were, in reality, a very big departure from the American political status quo. Sanders talk of socialism was not a call for a centrally-planned economy, but just for some European-style welfare state reforms. Trump's nationalism and derogatory words for certain demographics is a far cry from fascism or Nazism. The sudden, unpredicted success of both political mavericks was based on an extreme dissatisfaction and a longing for "an outsider."

"You're on Your Own"

American political discourse has long been defined by liberalism. The ideals of the European enlightenment, expressed by John Locke, Immanuel Kant, and others, and applied by Washington, Jefferson, and Hamilton put the individual above all else. In a repudiation of feudalism, the revolutionaries of 1776 embraced "freedom" as the true value of America.

In economic terms, this has meant unrestricted capitalism. Unlike most western countries, the US government does not provide public healthcare to its citizens. American college students, even those who attend public universities, must pay for their education, and millions remain in debt for decades. Employment is not guaranteed, and social services for low-income families are limited.

The American economic mantra is "personal responsibility," i.e. "you're on your own." While the US has the richest of the rich, measurements of basic societal health show that many get left behind. The rates of infant mortality, life expectancy, and poverty are statistically much worse than other western industrialized countries. In social terms, American liberalism has meant an ever increasing break down of traditional structures. Religion is considered to be a personal matter, and government institutions are forbidden from expressing faith or invoking divine authority.

The US Supreme Court has declared same-sex marriage is a constitutional right. Now debates about whether or not bathrooms in elementary schools should be gender segregated have erupted across America.

The ideology of liberalism, which has escalated over the course of American history, prescribes for the citizen to be like Thomas Jefferson's ideal "yoeman"; alone, unmolested and unattached to others, free to "pursue happiness" on his own, with no obligation to society, to his family, to God, or to anyone else.

However, as the crisis of racial tension illustrates, "No man is an island." Americans can watch the exact same video recordings, yet a majority of whites will defend the police, while African Americans will see brutality. Despite the obsessive individualism, Americans still identify themselves with groups they consider to be similar to themselves, and thus view the world accordingly.

Group identification is natural, and people have always had a collective nature. The entire history of humanity consists of humans cooperating, working together, agreeing on rules and expectations, and in the process, advancing civilization toward greater heights.

Liberalism & The American Dream

A severe lack of collective identity is very apparent in present day America. Items considered to be "public property" are in severe decay. The system of public transportation in Washington DC made national headlines when it shut down for a single day because of continued accidents, which had resulted in injuries and a single fatality.

Throughout 2016, accidents plagued the Amtrak public train system, which like DC transit system, also faces a lack of funding. During the 2016 academic year, millions of children have been left without schools to attend, as their for-profit charter schools, run by corporations, which have replaced public schools in many cities, have closed down mid-semester.

In the states that ultimately secured Trump's victory (Wisconsin, Michigan, Ohio, and Pennsylvania) one can find numerous neighborhoods that were once prosperous, now filled with empty, foreclosed homes. The factories that once employed millions of American industrial workers have closed their doors. The jobs that have replaced them offer much lower pay, to a generation which is unlikely to see the once lauded "American dream" of middle class prosperity.

Suicide rates across the United States are rising, as are cases of mental illness. Polls show that Americans increasingly find a lack of meaning and purpose in their lives, as their TVs and iPhones push them to purchase more and more, and live in pursuit of short-term pleasures. Economic security is also in question, as employment is far more short term for young workers, while the cost of housing and other living expenses are rising.

The changing political stage and rising instability shows a desperation on the part millions who are dissatisfied. The widely acknowledged problems facing the country are simply not being addressed. As Trump is sworn in at the beginning of 2017, the attempts to resolve the escalating crisis will continue. The search for answers outside of standard political discourse is likely to continue as well.

APPENDIX I:

'PUTINISM' IN AMERICAN HISTORY

August 8th, 2015 - New Eastern Outlook

Many articles in the US press have speculated at length in an attempt to define a new ideology called "Putinism." The pieces serve as an attempt to fit Putin into an outdated Cold War narrative, as if some new ideology in the Russian Federation is playing the role that Marxism-Leninism once played in the Soviet Union, though the current Russian constitution forbids this.

The notable leaders of history are rarely ideologues. History judges people mainly by what they achieve, not what they write or say. As Chinese President Xi Jinping recently put it: "The worth of any plan is in its implementation."

Putin has continued to play a specific role in the history of his country and the world. It is in his role as a leader of Russia that we can really define "Putinism." However, when examining his achievements, Putin's role and methods are not so different from those utilized by some well loved leaders in the history of the United States.

What has Putin achieved?

The dismantling of the Soviet Union, presided over by the pro-western Wall Street puppets in the Yeltsin regime, had catastrophic consequences. Ripping apart the state-run planned economy cast Russia and the surrounding countries into desperate ruin throughout the 1990s. There had been almost 100% employment during the Soviet period, but soon millions of Russians found themselves unemployed, with little social safety net. The medical system of the country, which had been one of the best in the world during the Soviet era, also descended into chaos.

Other problems that had been almost nonexistent during the Soviet period, such as narcotics, sex trafficking, and terrorism, also re-emerged with a vengeance. Organized crime, with roots in the underground economy of the Soviet period, suddenly became titanic and lethal. As the life expectancy and standard of living dropped, millions of Russians fled the country.

The only group that benefited during this post-Soviet chaos was a small group dubbed the "oligarchs." The privatized industries and natural resources ended up in their hands, and they proceeded to loot the country with almost no governmental restraint. Many of the wealthiest Russian capitalists refused even to pay taxes, as the government seemed powerless to enforce even basic laws.

Meanwhile, takfiri Islamist forces in Chechnya, who had been funded by the United States and NATO to fight the Soviet Union, escalated their horrific killings, kidnappings, and mass murders. It was in this context that Vladimir Putin, a former KGB officer, stepped up to lead the country. He began to battle the oligarchs and restore order. He directed the courts to prosecute some of the richest people and enforce the law. He oversaw the expansion of government-owned oil and natural gas corporations.

In 2005, Putin launched the "National Priorities Project," using government funds to build up the country's education, healthcare, agriculture, and housing.

The results of Putin's policies have been tremendous for the average Russian. During the first eight years of the Putin administration, the average wage in Russia has more than doubled. Unemployment has been drastically reduced. The rate of poverty has been reduced to 14%.

While the United States is suffering from the horrors of de-industrialization, Russia has been rapidly re-industrializing. During the first eight years of the Putin administration, industrial output increased by 125%, with overall industrial expansion higher than 70%. By 2007, Russia's industrial output had reached the level of 1990, meaning after 17 years, Russia had finally been able to recover from the disastrous restoration of capitalism.

Between 2007 and 2014, the Russian Gross Domestic Product increased from $764 billion to $2096.8 billion. Putin has stabilized the country by standing up for everyday Russians against the rich and powerful. Polls in Russia show that upwards of 80% of Russians have a favorable view of Vladimir Putin.

It was recently announced that Russia's crude oil production has now reached the highest level since the Cold War. An article from the October 6th edition of the Wall Street Journal quotes John Browne, the CEO of BP describing Russia's economy saying "No country has come so far, in such a short space of time.

Internationally, Putin has united with China, ending the tragic divide that began with the 1961 "Sino-Soviet Split." Putin has embraced the Bolivarian movement of Latin America and expanded trade with Cuba, Venezuela, Bolivia, and

Ecuador. Russia has joined the BRICS initiative for a new currency, and has become a close ally of the Islamic Republic of Iran.

Putin has attempted to remain on friendly terms with the United States, many times meeting with US presidents and often speaking highly of the United States in his speeches. However, as Russia becomes more stable, the United States has become more hostile to it. NATO is rapidly expanding, and a virulently anti-Russian regime has been installed in Ukraine.

Currently, Putin is in the process of attempting to destroy the Islamic State, or ISIS, in Iraq and Syria. The United States and its allies in the Gulf States have poured billions of dollars into an attempt to facilitate the violent overthrow of the Syrian Arab Republic. ISIS, which sprang up in 2014, has its roots in the Free Syrian Army, the Al-Nusra Front, and other US-supported extremist organizations.

Putin has made clear the Syrian Arab Republic is the country's legitimate government, and that US-funded "regime change" is undesirable. Since the US toppled the governments of Afghanistan, Iraq, and Libya, the countries have only become more impoverished and unstable. While the United States continues to fund the anti-government militants, Putin seeks to help the Baath Arab Socialist Party restore order to Syria so the refugee and humanitarian crisis can end, and the entire region can become safer.

Fighting Slavery & the British Empire

Putin is absolutely Russian, and his style of leadership draws from the vibrant and unique history of his country. However, some key aspects of his leadership style are not foreign to the United States. Two leaders, Abraham Lincoln and Franklin Delano Roosevelt, could certainly be described as "Putinists," if such a thing as "Putinism" exists.

Lincoln led the Republican Party when it was considered to be a radical Third Party in the mid-1800s. The Republican Party had taken its name because of the French Revolution and the republican revolutions that swept Europe in 1848. The slogan of the Republicans was "Free Land, Free Labor, and Free Men." The Republican Party was the party of labor unions, abolitionists, small farmers, recent immigrants, and advocates of women's rights. The New York City Republican Party newspaper, the New York Tribune, hired Karl Marx as its London correspondent.

Much like Vladimir Putin, Abraham Lincoln took office not as a firebrand but as a compromiser and moderate. Lincoln was reluctant to run for public office, only agreeing to enter politics when persuaded by friends and admirers. As a Christian,

Lincoln was morally opposed to the practice of slavery, but he was not an "abolitionist" because he did not think that moving to directly outlaw the practice was practical in the existing political context. Like Putin, Lincoln did not rise to power looking for a fight. When a fight presented itself, however, he did not back down — and won the love of millions for his strength.

The response of the slave-owners to Lincoln's election was immediate hostility. Both the Russian oligarchs who oppose Putin and the slaveholders who opposed Lincoln had a powerful ally: Wall Street. Unlike the rising industrial capitalists, the financial elites of the New York Stock Exchange had a real material interest in continuing slavery, as they made profits from cotton exports and insuring slave ships and plantations.

When the southern plantation owners announced that they were seceding from the United States, Lincoln mobilized the country to fight against the slave-owners and restore economic and political order. Lincoln was not afraid to stand up to the bankers, and with his eloquent speaking style and brilliance as an organizer, he led a broad anti-slavery coalition to victory.

Lincoln, like Putin, was called a "tyrant" and "human rights violator." Lincoln suspended many civil liberties in the context of a violent insurrection directed by some of the wealthiest

US President Abraham Lincoln aligned with Russia and a popular mass movement to defeat the insurgent southern slaveholders, backed by Wall Street and the British empire.

people. Lincoln's famous "Emancipation Proclamation" abolishing slavery in the southern states was an Executive Order that did not follow constitutional procedure. In the 1864 presidential election, people living in states controlled by the slaveholders were not given an opportunity to vote against him.

When it appeared that the British Empire may enter the war in support of slavery, which saw as a source of cheap cotton for their emerging textile industry, the Russian Czar announced that he would defend the United States. The Russian navy sent two fleets to American waters in the Atlantic Ocean to defend the United States from a potential British attack. The Russian Empire had recently abolished a slave-like form of serfdom, and was eager to support the United States in a similar endeavor.

Like Putin, Abraham Lincoln was not a Marxist or a socialist, but was still highly critical of capitalism and happy to align with dedicated, trustworthy left-wingers and radicals. Lincoln honored labor unions as an essential element in a democratic society, saying "Thank God we live under a system where men have the right to strike!" at the famous Lincoln-Douglas debate. Lincoln utilized the labor unions and craft guilds as key in strengthening the Union Army and its war effort. Lincoln happily accepted the endorsement of the International Workingmen's Association in the 1864 election, with his office sending a letter of gratitude directly to Karl Marx in London. Lincoln's army, which defeated the slaveholders, had among its highest ranks many self-described communists such as General August Willich and Colonel Joseph Weydemeyer.

The language currently used by the Wall Street media of the United States to describe Vladimir Putin is very similar to that used by the pro-slavery press and historians of the United States and Britain to describe Lincoln. Long after the Civil

War, Hollywood films like "Gone With The Wind" and "The Birth of a Nation" demonized Lincoln and glorified the southern slavocracy. Regardless of all who have worked to malign him, Lincoln is still widely remembered as one of the greatest presidents in US history. He may have initially been a reluctant abolitionist, even consciously racist — but history assigned him the position of the "Great Emancipator" and he fulfilled it tremendously.

Resisting
"Government By Organized Money"

In 1933, Franklin Delano Roosevelt took office, much like Putin, with his country in a state of economic ruin, reeling from the after-effects of the 1929 stock-market crash. Roosevelt's inaugural address made clear who was to blame, decrying the "unscrupulous practices" of high finance. Like Putin, Roosevelt mobilized the government sector to rescue the economy. Roosevelt passed the Glass-Steagall Act, preventing bankers from gambling with other people's money. Roosevelt began heavily taxing the wealthiest people in the United States, using the funds to hire the unemployed.

Similar to Xi Jinping's vision of the "New Silk Road," which Putin has fully cooperated with, Roosevelt's vision for economic development in the United States involved massive government-funded construction. During the Roosevelt Administration, post offices were built across the country. Hydro-electrical power plants were also constructed. The government subsidized the "National Theater Project," providing entertainment to schoolchildren and low-income people.

The unemployed youth hired into the Works Progress Administration wore bright green uniforms. They were not treated as "moochers" or "bums" for seeking government employment in a time of economic crisis, but rather as heroes, patriotically working for the good of the country. Towns often honored the "Boys in Green" with big parades as they arrived to pave the local roads, carve out parks, and otherwise beautify and develop the heartland of the United States.

Much like the opposition to Putin in Ukraine, the big bankers funded an openly pro-Hitler and

Just as Putin faces opposition from fascists in Ukraine, US President Franklin Roosevelt faced an attempted military coup in 1934 by admirers of Hitler. Roosevelt aligned with the Communist-led People's Front.

fascist movement against Roosevelt. Much like the Right Sector and the Avoz Battalion in the Ukraine, the American Liberty League, the Silver Legion of America, the German-American Bund, and the America First Committee were led by unapologetic Nazis. They saw repressive military dictatorship as favorable to Roosevelt's plan of mobilizing the people and consciously organizing the economy. In 1933, US Marine Corp General Smedley Butler revealed the infamous "business plot." Wall Street bankers had approached him about leading a military coup and forcibly deposing Roosevelt.

However, any attempted coup against Roosevelt would have failed, because like Putin, Roosevelt was loved by the everyday people of his country. Roosevelt's allies were not in corporate boardrooms, but on picket lines, hunger marches, and sit-down strikes. Roosevelt aligned himself with the "People's Front" coalition of socialists, communists, liberals, and progressives. When sit-down strikers occupied their Flint Michigan auto plant in 1937, Roosevelt sent in the army to protect the strikers from the local police and company thugs.

Like Lincoln, Roosevelt rejected Russophobia and did not want to pursue a deadly conflict with a huge Eurasian power. Roosevelt recognized and established diplomatic relations with the Soviet Union in 1935. His closest advisors like Joseph

Davies went to the Soviet Union and studied the "Five-Year Plans" which were rapidly industrializing the country. Roosevelt and famed physicist Niels Bohr worked hard, but were unable to convince Winston Churchill to back down and allow the Soviet Union to join the Manhattan Project.

Roosevelt was not a communist, but he had a clear understanding of problems of capitalism and the need to restrain the wealthy elite.

During his 1936 election campaign, he proclaimed: "Government by organized money is just as dangerous as government by organized mob." When Roosevelt went to greet textile workers in South Carolina, one of them famously shook his hand and said the president was "the first man in the White House to know that my boss is a son of a bitch." Prior to his death, Roosevelt proposed adding to the US Constitution a "New Bill of Rights" that would ensure everyone the right to jobs, housing, and healthcare.

Though Roosevelt had a big heart and deep love for working people, he was not afraid to lead them into battle. From 1941 to 1945, the United States stood shoulder to shoulder with the Soviet Union, the Chinese Communist Party's "Red Army," the peoples of Britain and France, and the armed partisan resistance groups in Japan, Germany, and Italy. Roosevelt and his political allies were always clear that fascism and its wealthy sponsors were far dangerous to the national security of the United States than were the peoples of Russia or China.

Roosevelt, like Lincoln and Putin, has been widely maligned. Half a century after his death, the likes of Glenn Beck still describe him as a "socialist" and a "traitor." However, like Lincoln, Roosevelt is still widely popular among the people. During his lifetime, Roosevelt was more popular than any other US president had ever been. After Roosevelt's 1945 death, term limits were added to the US constitution, preventing anyone else from being elected as US president four consecutive times.

Will American "Putinism" Re-Emerge?

It seems that just months ago, Barack Obama was lecturing the world about the evils of ISIS in order to justify his drone strike program and violations of Syria's territorial integrity. However, now that Vladimir Putin has escalated his support for the legitimate Syrian government which is scoring real victories against the ISIS menace, Obama is filled with outrage.

The reality is that the wealthy ruling class of the United States has no interest in defeating ISIS. The real objective of US policy in Syria since long before 2011 has always been to overthrow the

Syrian Arab Republic, a stable, anti-imperialist country with a heavily planned economy. ISIS originated as a faction among the anti-government terrorists who were funded by the United States and its Gulf State allies. While ISIS and the US may officially be enemies, Washington and its allies still fund the terrorists in Al-Nusra, and the Israeli government provides medical care to ISIS and other takfiris.

The supposed anti-ISIS airstrikes carried out by the US have been virtually meaningless, and were done without the permission of the Syrian government. Obama had attempted to justify airstrikes against the Syrian government a year earlier in response to allegations of chemical weapons, but failed to convince the international community. The US continues to openly call for the overthrow of the Syrian government, which controls the territory in which 80% of Syria's population is currently living, and was recently re-elected in a nationwide vote.

Unlike US and Turkish airstrikes, Russia's intervention in Syria is done with the full cooperation of the Syrian state. It cannot be described as "imperialism" or "foreign intervention." The Russian military is assisting the Syrian Arab Army as it battles a barrage of foreign terrorists, imported to their country with the help of Saudi Arabia, Jordan, Turkey, Qatar, France, Britain, and the United States.

Will a figure like Vladimir Putin emerge within the United States to resolve the prolonged political and economic crisis? Only time will tell.

Russia is not alone in wanting to defend the Syrian Arab Republic and smash the scourge of takfiri terrorism, created by the United States and its Gulf State allies. China is sending its forces to Syria. Hezbollah fighters are standing with the Syrian government. Communist Party militias and armed Christian brigades have been formed in Syria. Germany has even announced that it is happy to work with the Syrian government as well as Russia, Iran, China, and other countries to remove the scourge of ISIS.

Just as 70 years ago, a real united front of anti-fascists was formed to defeat the Wall Street-spawned scourge of Nazism, Russia is at the center of a broad coalition to defeat the oil bankers' latest monstrosity.

Christians, Islamists, communists, Baathists, and Russian nationalists are coming together and cooperating against a common foe. Putin is a leader who is rallying the world around the battle to improve peoples' livelihoods, defeat terrorism, and stand up to the source of so much evil, the wealthy global banking elite.

Such qualities of leadership currently displayed by Putin are not foreign to US shores, and if things in the country are to improve, those qualities must emerge in some form once again. Another leader of the caliber of Roosevelt, Lincoln, and Putin is desperately needed in the United States. A mass movement against the crimes of the rich, one that can produce and support such a leader, as the country and world become even more dangerous, is the greatest necessity of the hour.

Not only is the phenomenon widely described as "Putinism" not foreign to the United States. It is likely to return.

APPENDIX II:
THE FIGHT WITHIN U.S. BORDERS

Remarks at the Third International New Horizon Conference in Tehran on October 29, 2015.

It is not enough to be against racism, or to say you are against racism. Token anti-racist statements are everywhere in US society. Though Martin Luther King, Jr. was shot down and killed for his brave and dedicated work, after his death he has been reduced to a harmless patriotic icon. Even though the FBI worked to destroy him, schoolchildren across the US are taught that King's life is proof that the United States is "the greatest nation on earth."

The truth, and most people here are already aware, is that the United States is not a nation. The US is a country and within its borders are both oppressed and oppressor nations. African Americans, brought to the country as slaves, constitute an oppressed nation within US borders.

A lot of people in the United States say they are revolutionaries these days. Figures like Bernie Sanders show that radical-sounding words have become rather trendy. I say that you are not a revolutionary unless you recognize that Black people constitute a nation, and as a nation, have the right to self-determination, to choose separation or integration for themselves.

Trouble in "The Real America"

Every time I come to this part of the world, I meet so many young people who have a completely delusional portrait of the United States. What young Iranians see on satellite television — this portrait of the United States as a kind of rich paradise — this image is not real. If you watch US media, 90 percent of the time you are seeing southern California or New York City. The United States is far bigger than that.

In the heartland of the United States, what Sarah Palin demagogically called "the real America," there are millions of young people who are very unhappy. The US economy has been wrecked by deindustrialization. The steel mills, auto plants, and good-paying industrial jobs have been eliminated. The public sector jobs in teaching, libraries, and post offices have also been eliminated. Millions of young Americans are stuck in low-wage, short-term service-sector jobs, making a mere fraction of what their parents had in the much heralded "American middle class."

Young Americans watch the same garbage propaganda as is broadcast into Iran. They see how Kim Kardashian, the Real Housewives of New Jersey, and other wealthy people on American television live, and they contrast it to their own lives. The rates of suicide, mental illness, and drug addiction among young Americans are rising. They have been told all their lives that "you are worthless unless you are rich," and they now look into the future, realizing that they are likely to spend their lives far poorer than previous generations.

US society, born in racism, slavery, and the slaughter of indigenous people, is now entering a deep political and economic crisis. What's true is not always obvious — but in some cases it is. The US, in which there is another mass shooting every time you turn around, is not a healthy, moral society. It is not a model that any country should aspire to be like.

The Unfinished Revolution

The most hopeful period in the history of the United States was the direct aftermath of the Civil War. The Civil War was really the Second American Revolution. Abraham Lincoln led a beautiful coalition. It included Christian abolitionists, labor unionists, industrial capitalists, and most importantly, the enslaved African people.

When the war broke out, slaves throughout the south stopped working, in what constituted a mass general strike. Harriet Tubman became the first woman to lead US soldiers into battle, and she organized guerrilla bands, freeing slaves along the Combahee River in South Carolina.

The slaveocracy, aligned with the British Empire, was also supported by the Wall Street financial elite. They saw cotton exports from slave plantations as a way to make profits. But Wall Street, the British Empire, and the slave-owning aristocracy was defeated. They were defeated by an amazing alliance.

The Republican Party of the 1860s, far different than today, was a revolutionary party. It took its name from the French Revolution. It represented the small farmers, the African Americans, and the labor unions. For a brief period after the war, there was even talk of redistributing the land of slave owners.

Calling themselves the "Populists," the small farmers and free Blacks called for public control of railroads and guaranteed education for all, along with the overthrow of those they called "the monopolists": the wealthy bankers that had so much power.

The progressive coalition that came out of the Civil War was broken apart by Wall Street. What did they use to destroy this progressive, anti-capitalist mass movement? Racism.

The Ku Klux Klan began to use terrorist tactics, very similar to those currently used by the Israeli settlers, to violently force free Blacks out of the political process. Federal troops were pulled out of the south and it was handed back to the racists.

The Low-Wage Police State

Since that time, the white people of the United States have made a deal with Satan. As the big bankers have plundered the world, and used bombs, sanctions, and cruise missiles to beat down those who would assert their independence, we went along with it, we waved the flag. We were loyal and obedient, and in exchange we got houses, cars, and TV sets. We were taught to identify with Wall Street, and look down on the people of the world — and the Black and Brown people within the United States.

But the devil does not keep his promises. The "middle class" — the bribe given to white Americans to buy their obedience — is being gradually eliminated. The standard of living in the

United States is rapidly dropping. The civil liberties so often bragged about by US leaders are being stripped away. The US is rapidly transitioning to a low-wage police state.

The US economy has become centered on destruction. Prisons for profit, police on every corner, empty foreclosed homes, gentrification, rampant military aggression — war, war, war across the world.

As we face the ruins of US society, now it is time for white people to change the way we see ourselves. The satanic cabal of wealthy billionaires that has committed so many crimes around the world is our enemy. We must become friends with the people of Iran, Venezuela, Cuba, Russia, China, Palestine, and Yemen.

A new revolutionary coalition must be forged. An alliance of those within US borders who reject the rule of the globalist bankers can function as the US division of the emerging worldwide axis of resistance.

Every day the US government provides $18 million to the Israelis, as they escalate their genocidal crimes and provocations. A mass people's movement could demand that this money instead be spent on providing healthcare, jobs, and education to the next generation of people in the United States.

Thousands of US troops are stationed in military bases throughout this region. A mass peoples' movement could demand that these troops be brought home, and put to work restoring the crumbling roads and bridges throughout the United States.

The Task of Revolutionaries in the United States

The United States is currently facing very hard times, but as has often been said, "hard times are fighting times." The moment is approaching when a real people's movement against the racist Wall Street financial elites — their wars, their racism, their police state, and their global system of usury and poverty — can broadly expand within US society.

Such a people's movement will require solid unity of diverse political forces, concrete practical demands, and a clear vision of an entirely new society in North America.

Often in the United States, we are told that people who fight for their independence around the world are terrorists. If you want to know what terrorism is really about, go see the next Hollywood superhero movie. In this most American genre of films, we see a young white man who thinks the police aren't doing enough, so he puts on a cap and mask, and engages in isolated acts of violence. This is the Ku Klux Klan.

When Supreme Leader Khamenei says that ISIS and the police of the United States are the same, he is pointing to the fact that they utilized isolated acts of very publicized brutal violence in order to terrify a population. The Israeli settlers are doing the same thing.

Revolutionaries are not terrorists. They don't seek to terrify people and make them feel powerless. Great revolutionary leaders like Imam Khomeni, Malcolm X, and Eugene Debs are great not because of isolated acts they do themselves, but because they empower other people, pushing them ahead to achieve things they never even thought they were capable of doing.

We are entering a period of great potential for those in the US who are willing to fight for justice and equality. This conference is part of strategizing and building for the important struggles ahead.

APPENDIX III:

80 YEARS AGO, WHEN A BULGARIAN COMMUNIST SHOOK THE WORLD

A previously unpublished article written on the 80th anniversary of the Seventh World Congress of the Communist International.

On August 2, 1935, a speech was given in Moscow that would change history forever. The words spoken by a Bulgarian communist -- who had recently been released by Nazi jailers -- pushed millions of dedicated, disciplined activists into action, driving them to take on an untold number of heroic and self-sacrificing actions. The speech, since that time largely unknown and rarely referenced even in communist circles, was a pivotal moment in world history. The speech had an immeasurable impact on the events of the following decade, especially the Second World War.

The 1935 gathering where the address was given was the Seventh World Congress of the Communist International. The audience was a mere 600 people. The crowd in attendance, though small, represented leftist organizations in 65 countries, with 400 official delegates and 200 secretaries. The delegates in attendance represented 3,148,000 card-carrying communist party members from almost every corner of the globe. Soviet Premier Joseph Stalin sat prominently at the front of the meeting. A delegation of revolutionaries from the United States, including William Z. Foster, Earl Browder, and San Francisco Longshore Union Activist Sam Darcy was in the audience as well.

Georgi Dimitrov, International Anti-Fascist Celebrity

The speaker was Georgi Dimitrov, a middle-aged Bulgarian communist. Dimitrov had fled political persecution in his homeland, living much of his life as a professional revolutionary. With direction from Moscow, he had traveled across Europe, helping to coordinate and organize peace demonstrations, strikes, armed uprisings, and other legal and illegal activities intended to advance the cause of working class power.

In 1933, Dimitrov was rounded up along with German communists on orders of the country's new chancellor, Adolph Hitler. The excuse for the massive crackdown on dissent, along with the roundup of communists and socialists, had been the burning of the German parliament building known as the Reichstag. When Dimitrov was arrested, the Nazis claimed Dimitrov was the mastermind behind the Reichstag fire, and that he had been working on orders from the Soviet Union. After his arrest, Dimitrov had been given a huge public trial, staged for the purpose of justifying upcoming Nazi attacks on the Soviet Union.

At the highly publicized trial, things had gone far from the way the Nazis intended. Dimitrov, representing himself in what was supposed to be a kangaroo court, had humiliated his captors. He ripped Nazi leader Hermann Goering to shreds on the witness stand. Before a gallery of international observers it had become clear that Dimitrov had nothing to do with the crime he was accused of. Against all odds, through his acute skills of public speaking in his non-native German, Dimitrov was acquitted and released. He was granted passage to the Soviet Union, where he was welcomed as a hero.

Now an international celebrity, Dimitrov became a top leader of the Communist International (Comintern). At the historic 1935 gathering, it was Dimitrov who gave the keynote address. Many were surprised that Stalin did not take the podium himself, but gave the important task of delivering the primary political address to the Bulgarian anti-fascist hero. This may have been a strategic decision on Stalin's part, as the speech represented a big shift in the tactics of the communist movement.

Defining the Enemy, Mobilizing Resistance

The speech that so drastically changed the world 80 years ago began with a controversial thesis: a definition of fascism itself. While many leftists and academics saw fascism as an expression of middle class alienation, or the rule of a new "managerial class," Dimitrov rejected these notions. He declared, "Fascism is the power of finance capital itself. It is the organization of terrorist vengeance against the working class and the revolutionary section of the peasantry and intelligentsia. In foreign policy, fascism is jingoism in its most brutal form, fomenting bestial hatred of other nations."

Analyzing why the repressive, autocratic regimes had seized power in Italy and Germany, and why a global fascist movement was on the march, he proclaimed, "The imperialist circles are trying to shift the whole burden of the crisis onto the shoulders of the working people. That is why they need fascism. They are trying to solve the problem of markets by enslaving the weak nations, by intensifying colonial oppression and repartitioning the world anew by means of war. That is why they need fascism. They are striving to forestall the growth of the forces of revolution by smashing the revolutionary movement of the workers and peasants and by undertaking a military attack against the Soviet Union -- the bulwark of the world proletariat. That is why they need fascism."

Despite the wide implications and definitive ideological aspects of these words, it wasn't Dimitrov's analysis of the world situation that made his speech so important. The reason Dimitrov's speech changed the world so drastically was because of what followed. Dimitrov went on to call for a shift in the very style of activism taken on by the global movement of communists.

At the previous World Congress of the Comintern in 1928, the communist leaders had declared that social democrats were in fact "social fascists." With a tactical orientation called "United Front From Below" communists formed separate "red unions" and were urged to avoid alliances with non-communist elements. The time between 1928 and 1935 was referred to as the "Third Period," and the Communist international treated Social Democrats and non-communist reformists as the main enemy.

Dimitrov's speech, and the rest of the resolutions and presentations at the Seventh World Congress, urged the communists of the world to completely re-orient their tactics. Dimitrov urged communists to build "United Fronts Against Fascism" with social democrats, middle class reformers, and other left-wing elements. The United Front Against Fascism was to be part of a bigger "People's Front" in defense of democracy and against the drive for fascist dictatorship. Dimitrov explained that the "People's Front" would be open to everyone: "The Communist International puts no conditions for unity of action except one… that the unity of action be directed against fascism, against the offensive of capital, against the threat of war, against the class enemy. This is our condition."

The tactic of go-it-alone global general general strikes and uprisings was abandoned. The new policy, cemented with Dimitrov's speech, said that every possible alliance should be made, and every possible effort undertaken, to defeat the fascist menace. No more were the Social Democrats to be treated as sellout traitors. No more were anarchists to be dubbed as "dangerous ultra-lefts." "Unity of action" meant bringing the global anti-capitalist movement together.

Furthermore, anti-fascist elements among the capitalist class were to be embraced. Bourgeois democracy was far superior to fascist dictatorship, and principled alliances with capitalists on these grounds were now acceptable.

Directing Millions of Activists

Following Dimitrov's historic address, the world communist movement swung into action. This was no small turn of events. Becoming one of the 3,148,000 card-carrying communists in the world at this time was not a matter of simply agreeing with the party platform. Communist party members were required to give "the whole of their lives." They were required to abide by strict policies of democratic centralism, and in many countries, almost militaristic discipline.

For each of the millions of full Communist Party members in the world, there scores of people on communism's periphery. It is estimated that well over 90% of communist sympathizers never actually joined their country's respective communist party. Party membership was reserved only for the vanguard -- those who would put revolutionary activity first and all other matters in life second, and would faithfully carry out every task assigned to them.

The strength of the global communist movement had already shaken the world in the earlier part of the decade. International Unemployment Day on

March 6, 1930; the series of annual May 1 general strikes; many coordinated "days of action" -- all resulted in massive unrest across Europe and the United States. The world communist movement, with its network of unemployment councils, "red unions," and its League Against War and Fascism, was a real force to be reckoned with, capable of effectively impacting world politics. Dimitrov's speech put this well-oiled political machine into motion, with the primary task of destroying fascism.

The Global People's Front

In France, the new orientation led communists to hold a joint general strike with the socialists and anarchists in response to an attempted fascist coup. Eventually, a French "People's Front" government was elected.

In Spain, the People's Front policy led communists to lead an armed struggle to defend the Republic from General Francisco Franco. Communists from around the world volunteered and formed international brigades to fight the fascist insurgency. The Abraham Lincoln Brigade of the United States included thousands of young men and women who risked their lives in Spain to defend the Republic. The young revolutionaries from the US who travelled to Spain to fight fascism did so in open violation of the federal "Neutrality Act" and risked going to prison.

In Britain and many other countries, communists organized street battles against fascist thugs. At the famous "Battle of Cable Street" in 1936, a huge, broad, multinational crowd of working class people shut down a pro-Nazi rally from taking place in a Jewish neighborhood in London. The slogan communists rallied around to fight the fascists was "You Shall Not Pass" or "No Pasaran." The slogan had begun in Spain, and soon spread across the globe.

In the United States, the movement to build a "People's Front" led communists to the center of broad coalitions of progressive artists, musicians, trade unionists, academics, and anti-racists. The face of the People's Front in the United States was writers like Langston Hughes and Richard Wright, musicians like Woody Guthrie and Pete Seeger, and radical labor leaders like Harry Bridges.

Successes & Failures

Not everyone in the radical movement thought the "People's Front" was the best choice of action. Leon Trotsky declared that the Seventh World Congress proved the communist parties of the world to be "Menshevik" and "reformist." He formed his own "Fourth International" in response to it. Many writers have argued that the military defeat of the Spanish Republic took place because the working class was held back by its tight alliance with "democratic" capitalists.

Many Black activists and intellectuals felt the glorification of patriotism and US history concealed the ugly realities of racism and segregation. Other leftists disliked how in 1936, the Communist Party urged its members not to vote for their candidate Earl Browder, but instead to focus on reelecting Roosevelt and defeating the Republicans and their pro-Hitler allies in the "American Liberty League."

Michel Aflaq, a popular writer in the Middle East, drifted away from Marxism in response to the People's Front. He felt that the emphasis on anti-fascism made the communists too soft on the supposedly "democratic" imperialists like France and Britain. Aflaq went on to found the movement of Ba'ath Arab Socialism which eventually took power in Iraq and Syria. Regardless of the widespread criticism of the Comintern's policies and its possible shortcomings, the period from Dimitrov's speech until the defeat of the Axis powers in 1945 is remembered as a glorious moment of strength for the world communist movement.

In 1937, Communist Party-led autoworkers in Flint Michigan won union recognition with a sit-down strike. As they marched out of their plant, it was the single Black worker in the General Motors factory who carried the US flag. No one can deny the bold anti-racism of such an action in the age of Jim Crow, despite the patriotic imagery.

In the United States, the Communist Party's activism effectively linked Nazism and Italian fascism with the Ku Klux Klan and Jim Crow segregation in much of the public mind. The People's Front, despite softening any criticism of the Democrats and even scaling back a lot of southern activism, helped deal an ideological blow to racism. The young Rosa Parks, Paul Robeson, and millions of other African Americans saw the Communist Party's activist periphery as a good place to work effectively against racism.

With the popular front policy in Italy, France, and Germany, Communist Party members organized underground resistance groups. They bombed railroad tracks, sabotaged military production, and assassinated fascist leaders. When underground communist fighters faced the firing squads, they raised their fists in the classic communist salute and screamed "Stalin!" at the top of their lungs, reminding the captors of their bold and widely feared leader. After World War Two, the communist parties of France and Italy surged in membership due to the notoriety of their underground anti-fascist activism.

In China, the policies beginning with the Seventh World Congress allowed for Mao Zedong to temporarily form an alliance with Chiang Kai-Shek against the Japanese invaders. Over the course of the "War of Anti-Japanese Resistance," the Chinese communists and their Eighth Route Army won the hearts and minds of millions of Chinese people. The victory of the People's Republic came a mere four years after the lengthy "United Front" with the US-backed nationalists ended.

Fascism, Austerity & Resistance in the 21st Century?

So, other than the 80-year anniversary, why is Dimitrov's 1935 speech at all relevant in 2015? Well, far-right political parties are growing all across Europe. Golden Dawn, an organization of unapologetic Hitler worshippers has arisen in Greece. The French National Front, the British National Party, the UK Independence Party, and a slew of other groups are conducting mosque invasions and other blatant attacks on Muslim and immigrant communities.

The rise of right-wing movements accompanies a general suppression of civil liberties from the mainstream of the political establishment. The NSA is listening to our phone calls, and US citizens can now be extra-legally executed in drone strikes. The prison at Guantanamo Bay remains open despite the election and re-election of a Democratic administration.

The current period is certainly not an exact replica of the 1930s by any stretch, but certain similarities are indisputable. Underlying the rise of authoritarianism and extreme right-wing politics is "austerity." An economic crisis is driving the elimination of the social safety net in Europe and the United States.

As protests against the power of big bankers and the excesses of policing agencies take place across the planet, there is nothing comparable to the world communist movement of the 1930s. Though protests are getting bigger and bigger, what's left of the western world's Marxist-Leninists are elderly, weak, and divided into a slew of competing factions and tendencies.

Here in the 21st century, who like Dimitrov can declare a "general line" at a meeting in Moscow and drive millions to conduct a coordinated campaign of activism? Beyond party-affiliated communists and socialists, the left is full of competing theories and analyses. Many of those alienated by the economic crises and the police state find their explanation in conspiracy theories about the Illuminati and the Freemasons. Many in the US military, the prison system, and elsewhere -- who in another era would have become adherents of Che Guevara and Mao Zedong -- are today becoming disciples of Alex Jones.

As a confused generation of young activists moves into action, confronting the police state and the economic crisis, there are without a doubt certain lessons that can be taken away from Dimitrov's groundbreaking lecture to the Seventh World Congress of the Communist International.

What lessons can be learned? What was done right? What went tragically wrong and why? This is what the next generation of fearless radicals must determine for themselves as they gear up for battle, 80 years later. The pre-written assumptions and narratives are proving themselves to be inadequate. It is now time for innovation and creativity in the face of global catastrophe.

However, innovation and creativity still require knowledge of what has taken place before. The history of the world communist movement, both its failures and achievements, simply cannot be forgotten.

Caleb Maupin has worked as a journalist and political analyst for the last five years. He has reported from across the United States, as well as from Iran, the Gulf of Aden and Venezuela. He has been a featured speaker at many Universities, and at international conferences held in Tehran, Quito, and Brasilia. His writings have been translated and published in many languages including Farsi, Chinese, Russian, Arabic, Spanish, and Portuguese. He is originally from Ohio.

CalebMaupin.info